HITCH YOUR WAGON TO A STAR

HITCH YOUR WAGON TO A STAR

And Other Quotations by RALPH WALDO EMERSON

Keith Weller Frome

Columbia University Press

New York

Columbia University Press

New York   Chichester, West Sussex

Copyright © 1996 Columbia University Press

All rights reserved

Library of Congress Cataloging-in-Publication Data

Frome, Keith.

  Hitch your wagon to a star and other quotations from Ralph Waldo
Emerson / Keith Weller Frome : with preface by Leslie Fiedler.

    p. cm.

  Includes index.

  ISBN 0–231–10372–7 (acid-free paper)

  1. Emerson, Ralph Waldo, 1803–1882—Quotations. 2. Quotations,
American. I. Emerson, Ralph Waldo, 1803–1882. II. Title.

PS1603.F76 1996

818'.302–dc20   95–47976

Printed in the United States of America

c 10 9 8 7 6 5 4 3 2 1

For Ermelinda

Contents

PREFACE

Ralph Waldo Emerson is, with the possible exception of Benjamin Franklin, the most quotable of all American writers. Indeed, as we read his works, the gnomic sentences of which they are composed tend to detach themselves from their original contexts and live on in our heads the independent life of popular aphorisms and anonymous nursery rhymes. This is scarcely surprising, since what we first encounter as complete essays and poems were cobbled together from just such fragmentary phrases scribbled down in Emerson's journals. What is surprising is that, despite Emerson's quotability, when Keith Frome proposed compiling this collection, he found that no similar volume was in print. Yet even this is explicable in light of Emerson's declining reputation at the end of the twentieth century, at which point—for reasons more ideological than esthetic—he had almost ceased to be read outside the classroom.

On the one hand, Marxist critics charged that his pseudolibertarian credo of self-reliance was in fact just another version of the code of rugged individualism, so dear to the hearts of American imperialists and Robber Barons. On the other, the self-styled "New Critics" condemned him for having denied the reality of Evil and the fallen nature of mankind. By the 1930s, when these two attacks had peaked, I was just finding my critical voice and stance, and I found myself influenced by both sides. Consequently, in the decades since, I have published much about almost the whole range of American literature and culture, but I have never dealt at length with Emerson.

Nonetheless, when asked to write a preface for this collection, I accepted without a moment's hesitation. It occurred to me, despite our ideological differences, resonant phrases from Emerson's long unread works had continued to echo and re-echo in my head. Not only had I, at age seventeen, inscribed next to my high school graduation picture "To be great is to be misunderstood," but a quarter of a century later I had headed the chapters of my first novel with tags like "Who drinks of Cupid's nectar cup/Loveth downward and not up . . ."

When I tried Emerson's text, however, I found I could still not reread any of his willfully incoherent essays with ease and pleasure. I did somewhat better with the poems, although when they exceed a certain length, they, too, tend to explode into what he himself called "infinitely repellent particles."

Since such centrifugal congeries of disparate images are more acceptable in rhapsodic verse than in didactic prose, I decided it was better to read even what purport to be essays as if they were poems—or rather, perhaps, anthologies of minipoems, requiring of us not belief but the willing suspension of disbelief.

There is, in any case, a good warrant for such a strategy, considering that Emerson, although he founded no continuing school of philosophy, directly inspired Walt Whitman and Emily Dickinson, whom we have come to consider our two greatest poets. Moreover, Emerson once unequivocally declared, "I am in all my theory, ethics and politics a poet." Sometimes he qualified this, writing once in a distancing third person, "He was a poet, though his singing was husky and for the most part in prose": to which James Russell Lowell was moved to add wryly, "No, 'tis not even prose."

What Emerson wrote was in fact neither "prose" nor "poetry," as defined by conventional household poets in the Victorian Era. Yet it was precisely his blurring of the distinction between the "poetic" and the "non-poetic" that made possible the more subversive and uniquely American experiments of Whitman and Dickinson. There is also a disconcerting lack of warmth in Emerson, however, that makes him unlike these eminent disciples; and of this, too, he was uneasily aware, confessing, "I was uncertain always whether I have one spark of that fire which burns in verse. . ." Herman Melville was certain that Emerson did *not*; in describing Mark Winsome, the wicked caricature of Emerson who appears in *The Confidence Man*, Melville calls him ". . .purely and coldly radiant as a prism. It seemed as if one could almost hear him vitreously chime and ring."

Yet, however frigidly, his sentences *do* chime and ring—thus producing in some auditors at least (as Melville seems not to have realized) the state of "ecstasy" that Emerson sought to evoke in print or from the lecturer's platform. As Robert Frost, the third and latest of Emerson's poetic disciples, reminds us in quite another context, ". . . Ice/is also great/and would suffice."

The present collection of such icily ecstatic phrases reminds us once more of this same disconcerting fact, thus posthumously adding a peculiarly American postscript to the secular scriptures that Emerson set out to compile at the beginning of his career. "No man," he wrote at that point, "could be better occupied than in making his own bible by harkening to all those sentences which now here, now there, now in nursery rhymes, now in Hebrew, now in English bards, thrill them like the sound of a trumpet. . ." Let us, therefore, harken again and be thrilled.

LESLIE A. FIEDLER
Buffalo, New York
July 26, 1995

$\mathcal{I}$NTRODUCTION

This book offers 750 quotations from the major works of Ralph Waldo Emerson arranged by subject, with the hope that Emerson's thoughts will be rescued from the arid corridors of the academy and be taken up anew by the interested, reflective man or woman who is engaged in the work of the day. Emerson devoted his lectures and essays to this kind of audience, and his lectures were always well attended. Yet today, if he is read at all, it is by the segregated, cloistered scholars and intellectuals he continually assails in his writings. He demanded the light of day for his ideas and willed them to provoke conversation in the marketplace as well as in the lecture hall or at the lyceum. An 1847 journal entry reads: "A Scholar is a candle which the love & desire of men will light. Let it not lie in a dark box." This collection is intended to reintroduce Emerson's ideas to the daylight and to the general public for whom his words were originally intended.

In his 1859 lecture "Quotation and Originality," Emerson said, "Next to the originator of a good sentence is the first quoter of it. Many will read the book before one thinks of quoting a passage. As soon as he has done this, that line will be quoted east and west." Although it seems as if Emerson is indeed quoted "east and west," I find it revealing that there does not exist an Emerson book of quotations in print. There are single-author quotation books in print devoted to William Shakespeare, Mark Twain, and Abraham Lincoln. In the realm of American letters, Emerson is at least as important as Twain and Lincoln and certainly as quotable. In fact, if we take as our barometer the three major quotations books, that is, *Bartlett's Familiar Quotations*, *The Oxford Dictionary of Quotations*, and *The Columbia Dictionary of Quotations*, Emerson could very well be nominated as the most quoted American writer. The latest edition of *Bartlett's* gives 147 selections from Emerson; the third edition of Oxford's book includes 45. *The Columbia Dictionary of Quotations* includes 200 Emerson selections. Emerson's comparatively small sampling in *The Oxford Dictionary of Quotations* is presumably due to an Anglocentric selection process. Proportionately, though, he is still the most significant American in Oxford's constellation, which includes only 28 quotations from Henry David Thoreau, 26 from Twain, 1 from Herman Melville, 28 from Henry James, and none from H. L. Mencken. In the Columbia collection, Emerson's likely American competitors fall far short: there are only 22

Lincoln quotations, 78 Ambrose Bierce quotations, 27 Melville quotations, 21 Nathaniel Hawthorne quotations, 97 F. Scott Fitzgerald quotations, and 58 H.L. Mencken quotations. Thoreau makes a serious run with 164 quotations, and Mark Twain weighs in with a respectable 154 excerpts, but both still are well behind Emerson. Indeed, in the assembly of witty and wise persons who constitute the Columbia book, Emerson is in the pantheon of the most quotable persons in the English language, along with Shakespeare, Samuel Johnson, Lord Byron, and Oscar Wilde.

But Emerson is not read much these days. And, as the philosopher Stanley Cavell has been pointing out for some time now, when Emerson is read, he is not handled with intellectual care or respect. The educated, general public, who compose the audience for this book, recognize that he is important, and perhaps feel that they ought to be more familiar with his works, but few have the time or take the time to wrestle with one of his essays. As high school and college literature curricula strive to include more and more historically neglected writers and traditions, this most American writer begins to fade. Even in my own school, which is a traditional boys school, Emerson is not studied in depth in our literature classes, and my own enthusiasm for him is regarded by the faculty as the quaint hobby of their too philosophical principal.

Nowhere does Emerson's neglect seem more symbolically salient than at Harvard Divinity School, where he was a student and where he later delivered the still controversial "Divinity School Address," one of the greatest articulations of the liberal theological vision. Today, Emerson's works are rarely taught at Harvard Divinity School. He is sneered at by a wide spectrum of students and professors there. Liberals take him to be the paradigmatic white, Western male thinker who celebrates such patriarchal, hierarchical values as separation and solitude. Conservatives blame him for contributing to the continued dissolution of organized religion, especially in the liberal Christian community. Some Unitarian scholars never tire of arguing that the decline of the Unitarian denomination and contemporary ignorance of its heritage by its dwindling congregations began with the "Divinity School Address." One even produced a defense of Barzillai Frost, the poor minister who serves as Emerson's whipping boy in the Address.

Harvard students can go through their years at the Divinity School without reading a sentence from Emerson, save for the quotation on the bronze plaque commemorating the "Divinity School Address" in the Divinity Hall Chapel. The plaque gives the date of the address and quotes from it: "Acquaint thyself at first hand with Deity." When I was a student at The Divinity School, I heard this sentence used time and again to show either that Emerson supported disjunction and solitude (i.e., we find God alone, separated and disconnected) or that he sought to annihilate the structure and polity of the institutional church (i.e., "thyself" is emphasized, therefore disregarding the need for ministers or traditions). None noticed, however, that the plaque misquotes the passage from the Address. The actual sentence reads: "Yourself a newborn bard of the Holy Ghost,—cast behind you all conformity, and acquaint men at first hand with Deity." The correct sentence directs you as the minister to embrace your congregation and, through your character and works, introduce it to the immediacy of the Divine. Rather than reject your parish and the world of humanity, Emerson calls for you to join them in the daily search for revelation. The plaque still hangs in the chapel, uncorrected.

It should be corrected because getting Emerson right often depends on paying close attention to his exact word choices in a sentence. Each word implies a summary of Emerson's philosophical project, which is to bridge the individual and the universal without losing the identity of either. As he says in his essay "The Poet": "Every word was once a poem. Every new relation is a word." When you read "men" instead of "thyself" the entire meaning of the passage on the plaque changes. The idea of coming to know the Divine in a direct intimate, personal, and individual way is retained, but the image of community—that is, of one person (the minister/poet) helping others on the way—is also asserted. Hence the correct word transforms the light of the sentence, and brings us closer to the heart of Emerson's basic philosophical quest, which is to envision a community of provocateurs who through their relationships inspire not conformity but a sort of connected individualism. Emerson's biographer, Robert D. Richardson, Jr., has called Emerson's notion of community "a voluntary association of fulfilled individuals."[1] Reading "men" instead of "thyself," as a matter of fact, brings us a step closer to understanding Emerson's epistemic enterprise: to see the universe as a collection of interrelated symbols, of which the individual person is one. In Emerson's vision, the universe can be discovered in the individual as the eternal can be discovered in the transient, the extraordinary in the ordinary. This connection between the transcendent and the immanent and the human self is expressed in Emerson's familiar maxim that the further in one goes the further out one comes. The soul is a symbol for nature, and nature symbolizes the individual soul. As Emerson puts it in "The Poet": "The Universe is the externisation of the soul" and "Things admit of being used as symbols because nature is a symbol, in the whole, and in every part."

There is, then, a philosophical justification for collecting quotations from Emerson's works. This book will indeed be useful to the person who wants to taste Emerson but doesn't have the time to take on one of the essays, or who wants to find the exact wording or location of one of his famous sayings, or who is searching for a profound insight on a particular topic. But a representative collection of Emerson's sentences is also a collection of Emerson's basic and best arguments. Scholars have debated whether Emerson's essays are merely sentences strung together or are tightly constructed, coherent compositions. Stanley Cavell has argued that Emerson can be regarded as the philosopher of the sentence. Cavell, I believe, is talking about a mode of writing and arguing, i.e., of doing philosophy. If you read any of Cavell's expositions of Emerson's epistemology, you find that Cavell's technique, as he says in the essay "Thinking of Emerson," is to lay sentences "beside" each other.[2] Reading Cavell's Emersonian excursions is like witnessing a woodsmen building a dwelling in the forest by laying planks and logs together from other abandoned cabins. In the same essay, Cavell describes Emerson's own mode of composition in a similar way, stating that his writing is a form of building a world to inhabit, "sentence by shunning sentence."

The tumult of sentences in an Emerson essay may be regarded as symbolic of the fluid goal of Emerson's theory of knowledge. Emerson seeks to receive the world rather than to clutch it, to provoke rather than to instruct, to commit to dwell in the everyday and the particular rather than to ascend in any final way to the abstract. Emerson seeks to acknowledge and live with the flux and flow of experiences in our daily life, rather than attempt to impose a final interpretation on them. This is why Cavell prods us, in his essay "Finding as Founding," to ponder the "look of Emerson's prose."[3] In an interview with the Italian philosopher Giovanna Borradori, Cavell said: "The Emersonian sentence is always a problem for any critic that looks at it. What are these sentences doing? Are they connected to one another? What's the topic sentence? *That they are each of them a universe* entails for me the investigation of the language to which this sentence is native"[4] (my emphasis.) It is in the very process of writing that Emerson seeks his philosophical and religious identity and stance, and this is why a collection of his best sentences makes not only a useful reference book, but one with a critical justification that goes beyond the location of witty and articulate ideas.

A collection of the best of Emerson's quotations allows us to concentrate on him at the sentence and at the word level. This can give us some idea as to how he makes his arguments. I am not proposing that Emerson's essays and lectures are superfluous as coherent compositions, or that they are merely strings of quotable sentences. But Cavell is correct, I believe, to ask us to investigate the relationship of *all* sentences in Emerson's essays and in all of his other writings. By saying that each of Emerson's sentences is a universe, I am asking the readers of this compilation to enter hundreds of universes and, in doing so, gain an introduction to the Emersonian worldview, where every ordinary word counts as crucial. This collection is true to Emerson's basic reflex to provoke rather than to instruct, for it is in his commitment to provocation as a vocation that Emerson escapes conformity and yet remains in conversation, or as he would put it, "truly speaking."

Contrary to popular opinion, Emerson is as concerned with the details of life as he is with the larger questions of death, God, and ultimate meaning. This collection reflects Emerson's dialectical oscillation between the happy and tragic particulars of everyday life and the more transcendental themes for which he is famous. In the following pages, Emerson will comment on Adolescence, Aging, Ambition, the Body, Books, Boys, Business and Commerce, Cathedrals, Cities, Company, Common People, Conversation, Courage, Drugs, Education, Eyes, Farming, Gifts, Government, Happiness, Heroes, Intellectuals, the Ministry, Morality, Parenting, Politics, Power, the Self, Silence, Slavery, Solitude, Success, Suffering, Teaching, Travel, Wealth, Work, and Writing (to name a few of the subjects) as well as his overarching themes of nature, God, spirituality, genius, greatness, conformity, inspiration and individualism.

At heart, Emerson was interested in the way we live our lives as Americans and how the quality of our individual lives would add up to create a new country. It is important that the American public continue to read Emerson, for he struggled to explore the moral and spiritual character of the United States, a search that we are still engaged in as our economy and demography rapidly change. The United States is the most adolescent of countries, for it seems that it is always in the process of an identity crisis. Severed by definition from tradition, and continually incorporating new peoples, the republic is in a constant and agitated state of renewal and self-definition. As we approach the millennium, spurred on by a fractious Congress and the omnipresent media, we continue to search for who we are. This quest for a national identity and mission is often tortured, sometimes violent, and rarely pleasant. The debates we see today in Congress about taxes, welfare, state rights, family, personal responsibility, school prayer, and government power are in one way or another conflicts over the identity of the country. We ask, as Emerson asked, what the appropriate relationship is between the individual and the community and the individual and the creation. We seek that delicate balance between individual freedom, self-reliance, and the individual's responsibility to his or her neighborhood, state, and country. We are still seeking to establish the Emersonian community of fulfilled individuals.

The essential question Emerson asked of America was about the status of the individual. In a way, all the quotations in this book are a variation of this question. Systematically unsystematic and conscientiously undogmatic,

Emerson grappled with several approaches. He was not an isolationist though he may seem that at times. He was not a strict communitarian, though there are Emersonian moments of sacrifice. His answer lay in a religious sense of self that was connected with the whole of creation and, at the same time, stood apart from the world, often as the sharing creator of that world. Now, more than ever, I recommend Emerson to America as a mentor to our national conversation about who we are and how we ought to treat ourselves and others and the environment and the cosmos. For to see it all intimately related, as through a transparent eyeball, is perhaps to start to mend the disenfranchised and fractured nature of our national and personal lives at this moment.

1. Robert D. Richardson, Jr. *Emerson: The Mind on Fire* (Berkeley: University of California Press, 1995), p. 322.
2. Cavell's exams in his course on Emerson in Harvard College consist of sentences from the assigned readings. The student is to pick two sentences and relate them to one another.
3. Stanley Cavell, "Finding as Founding," in *This New Yet Unapproachable America* (Albuquerque, NM: Living Batch Press, 1989), p. 116.
4. Giovanna Borradori, *The American Philosopher* (Chicago: University of Chicago Press, 1994), p. 133.

Sources

The original sources for the selections in this book can be found, for the most part, in:

The Complete Works of Ralph Waldo Emerson, 12 vols., ed. Edward W. Emerson. Boston: Houghton Mifflin, 1903–1904.

Other essential collections are:

Journals of Ralph Waldo Emerson, 10 vols., eds. E. W. Emerson and W. E. Forbes. Boston: Houghton Mifflin, 1909–1914.

The Letters of Ralph Waldo Emerson, 8 vols., eds. Ralph Rusk and Eleanor Tilton. New York: Columbia University Press, 1939–1991.

The Journals and Miscellaneous Notebooks of Ralph Waldo Emerson, 16 vols., eds. William H. Gilman et al. Cambridge: Harvard University Press, 1960–1982.

The Early Lectures of Ralph Waldo Emerson, 3 vols., eds. S. E. Whicher, R. E. Spiller and W. E. Wiliams. Cambridge: Harvard University Press, 1959–1972.

The Complete Sermons of Ralph Waldo Emerson, 4 vols., eds. Albert J. Von Frank, Ronald A. Bosco, Teresa Toulouse, and Andrew H. Delbanco. Columbia, MO: University of Missouri Press, 1989-.

If you are building a home library of Emerson's basic works, I suggest the following volumes:

1. *Emerson: Essay and Lectures*, ed. Joel Porte. New York: The Library of the Mind, 1983.
   -This handsome edition contains all of the essays as well as "Nature," "Representative Men," "English Traits," "The Conduct of Life," and several lectures including "The Divinity School Address," "The American Scholar," "Literary Ethics," "The Method of Nature," "Man the Reformer," "The Conservative," "The Transcendentalist," "The Young American," and "Introductory Lecture on the Times." Porte also reproduces several pieces of uncollected prose including, most notably, "The Lord's Supper."

2. *Emerson: Collected Poems and Translations*, eds. Harold Bloom and Paul Kane. New York: The Library of America, 1994.

-This edition includes all of *Poems, May-Day and Other Pieces,* and *Selected Poems* as well as poems Emerson published in magazines, his journals and his notebooks.

3. *Emerson in His Journals,* ed. Joel Porte. Cambridge: Harvard University Press, 1982.
   -Porte distills this vast amount of material to a one-volume representation of the heart of Emerson's journals. Arranged chronologically, this is one of the most entertaining and interesting of the Emerson primary sources.

4. Robert D. Richardson, *Emerson: The Mind on Fire.* Berkeley: University of California Press, 1995.
   -The most up-to-date and complete intellectual biography of Emerson available. Gay Wilson Allen's clear and readable *Ralph Waldo Emerson* (New York: Viking Press, 1981) is also very good. Joel Porte's *Representative Men: Ralph Waldo Emerson in His Time.* (New York: Columbia University Press, 1988) is a textual biography of Emerson that seeks to link his life with close readings of his works. Carlos Baker's *Emerson Among the Eccentrics* (New York: Viking, 1996) is an informative and well-written account of Emerson's friendships and the times within which he worked. Baker grapples with the basic Emersonian tension between society and solitude.

CTION

The one thing in the world, of value, is the active soul.

"The American Scholar," *Emerson: Essays and Lectures*, ed. Joel Porte (1983).

Oration, August 31, 1837, delivered before the Phi Beta Kappa Society, Cambridge, Massachusetts.

See also SOUL

This time, like all times, is a very good one, if we but know what to do with it.

"The American Scholar," *Emerson: Essays and Lectures*, ed. Joel Porte (1983).

Oration, August 31, 1837, delivered before the Phi Beta Kappa Society, Cambridge, Massachusetts.

The law of nature is, do the thing, and you shall have the power: but they who do not the thing have not the power.

"Compensation," *Essays*, First Series (1841, repr. 1847).

This is reminiscent of Emerson's advice in "Self-Reliance": "But do your thing and I shall know you." What is this "thing"? It might be argued that Emerson chooses such an ambiguous, open-ended word to concentrate the reader's attention on the verb "to do," for he is as much a philosopher of action as he is a theologian of contemplation.

See also POWER

Convert life into truth.

"The Divinity School Address," *The Portable Emerson*, ed. Carl Bode (1946, repr. 1981). Address, July 15, 1838, delivered before the senior class in Divinity College, Cambridge.

This is the epigram in the middle of a sentence that reads: "The capital secret of his profession, namely to convert life into truth, he had not learned." Here Emerson is criticizing an unnamed minister who Conrad Wright later convincingly argued to be Barzillai Frost, minister of the Concord Unitarian Church from 1837 to 1857. See Wright's *The Liberal Christians* (Unitarian Universalist Association, 1970, repr. 1980).

See also MINISTRY, THE

$\mathcal{A}$DOLESCENCE

The age of puberty is a crisis in the age of man worth studying. It is the passage from the unconscious to the conscious; from the sleep of passions to their rage.

The Journals and Miscellaneous Notebooks of Ralph Waldo Emerson, vol. 4, (1960–1978).

$\mathcal{A}$GE AND AGING

In youth, we clothe ourselves with rainbows, with hope & love, & go as brave as the zodiac. In age we put out another sort of perspiration; gout, fever, rheumatism, caprice, doubt, fretting, and avarice.

Emerson in His Journals, October-November 1849, ed. Joel Porte (1982).

It is time to be old,
To take in sail:—
The god of bounds,
Who sets to seas a shore,
Came to me in his fatal rounds,
And said: 'No more!'

"Terminus," May-Day and Other Pieces (1867).

Spring still makes spring in the mind,
When sixty years are told;
Love wakes anew this throbbing heart,
And we are never old.

"The World-Soul," Poems (1847).

$\mathcal{A}$LIENATION

We walk alone in the world. Friends, such as we desire, are dreams and fables.

"Friendship," Essays, First Series (1841, repr. 1847).

See also SOLITUDE

It is an odd jealousy: but the poet finds himself not near enough to his object. The pine-tree, the river, the bank of flowers before him, does not seem to be nature. Nature is still elsewhere.

"Nature," *Essays: Second Series* (1844).

See also POETRY AND POETS

*A*MBITION

Men seek to be great; they would have offices, wealth, power, and fame. They think that to be great is to possess one side of nature,—the sweet, without the other side,—the bitter.

"Compensation," *Essays*, First Series (1841, repr. 1847).

See also GREATNESS

Every young man is prone to be misled by the suggestions of his own ill-founded ambition which he mistakes for the promptings of a secret genius, and thence dreams of unrivaled greatness.

The Journals and Miscellaneous Notebooks of Ralph Waldo Emerson, vol. 2, (1960–1978).

See also YOUTH

*A*NGELS

The angels are so enamored of the language that is spoken in heaven, that they will not distort their lips with the hissing and unmusical dialects of men, but speak their own, whether there be any who understand it or not.

"Intellect," *Essays*, First Series (1841, repr. 1847).

See also LANGUAGE

*A*RCHITECTURE

I have heard that stiff people lose something of their awkwardness under high ceilings, and in spacious halls. I think, sculpture and painting have an effect to teach us manners, and abolish hurry.

"Culture," *The Conduct of Life* (1860).

See also SCULPTURE

ARISTOCRACY

The persons who constitute the natural aristocracy, are not found in the actual aristocracy, or, only on its edge; as the chemical energy of the spectrum is found to be greatest just outside of the spectrum.

"Manners," *Essays*, Second Series (1844).

See also CHARACTER

ART AND ARTISTS

Art is the need to create; but in its essence, immense and universal, it is impatient of working with lame or tied hands, and of making cripples and monsters, such as all pictures and statues are. Nothing less than the creation of man and nature is its end.

"Art," *Essays*, First Series (1841, repr. 1847).

See also CREATIVITY

Art should exhilarate, and throw down the walls of circumstance on every side, awakening in the beholder the same sense of universal relation and power which the work evinced in the artist, and its highest effect is to make new artists.

"Art," *Essays*, First Series (1841, repr. 1847).

The virtue of art lies in detachment, in sequestering one object from the embarrassing variety. Until one thing comes out from the connection of things, there can be enjoyment, contemplation, but no thought.

"Art," *Essays*, First Series (1841, repr. 1847).

See also THINKING AND THOUGHT

Always the seer is a sayer. Somehow his dream is told: somehow he publishes it with solemn joy: sometimes with pencil on canvas: sometimes with chisel on stone; sometimes in towers and aisles of granite, his soul's worship is builded; sometimes in anthems of indefinite music; but clearest and most permanent, in words.

"The Divinity School Address," repr. in *The Portable Emerson*, ed. Carl Bode (1946, repr. 1981).

Address, July 15, 1838, delivered before the senior class in Divinity College, Cambridge.

See also WORSHIP

Great is paint; nay, God is the painter; and we rightly accuse the critic who destroys too many illusions. Society does not love its unmaskers.

"Illusions," *The Conduct of Life* (1860).

See also GOD

A work of art is an abstract or epitome of the world. It is the result or expression of nature, in miniature. For, although the works of nature are innumerable and all different, the result or the expression of them all is similar and single.

Nature, ch. 3, (1836, revised and repr. 1849).

The eye is the best of artists.

Nature, ch. 3, (1836, revised and repr. 1849).

Art is a jealous mistress, and if a man have a genius for painting, poetry, music, architecture or philosophy, he makes a bad husband and an ill provider, and should be wise in season and not fetter himself with duties which will embitter his days and spoil him for his proper work.

"Wealth," *The Conduct of Life* (1860).

In the Greek cities, it was reckoned profane, that any person should pretend a property in a work of art, which belonged to all who could behold it.

"Wealth," *The Conduct of Life* (1860).

$\mathcal{A}$STROLOGY

The too much contemplation of these limits induces meanness. They who talk much of destiny, their birth-star, &c., are in a lower dangerous plane, and invite the evils they fear.

"Fate," *The Conduct of Life* (1860).

Astronomy to the selfish becomes astrology.

"Nature," *Essays,* Second Series (1844).

ASTRONOMY

It is noticed, that the consideration of the great periods and spaces of astronomy induces a dignity of mind, and an indifference to death.

"Culture," *The Conduct of Life* (1860).

The stars awaken a certain reverence, because though always present, they are inaccessible.

Nature, ch. 1, (1836, revised and repr. 1849).

See also CREATION, THE

AUTHENTICITY

The reason why any one refuses his assent to your opinion, or his aid to your benevolent design, is in you: he refuses to accept you as a bringer of truth, because, though you think you have it, he feels that you have it not. You have not given him the authentic sign.

"New England Reformers," *Essays*, Second Series (1844).

Lecture, March 3, 1844, in Amory Hall, Boston, Massachusetts.

See also TRUTH

The lesson which these observations convey is, be, and not seem. Let us acquiesce. Let us take our bloated nothingness out of the path of the divine circuits. Let us unlearn our wisdom of the world. Let us lie low in the lord's power, and learn that truth alone makes rich and great.

"Spiritual Laws," *Essays*, First Series (1841, repr. 1847).

See also TRUTH

BANKS

For you, o broker, there is no other principle but arithmetic. For me, commerce is of trivial import; love, faith, truth of character, the aspiration of man, these are sacred; nor can I detach one duty, like you, from all other duties, and concentrate my forces mechanically on the payment of moneys.

"Circles," *Essays*, First Series (1841, repr. 1847).

See also BUSINESS AND COMMERCE

*B*EAUTY

Though we travel the world over to find the beautiful, we must carry it with us, or we find it not.

"Art," *Essays*, First Series (1841, repr. 1847).

See also TRAVELING AND TRAVELERS

And yet—it is not beauty that inspires the deepest passion. Beauty without grace is the hook without the bait. Beauty, without expression, tires.

"Beauty," *The Conduct of Life* (1860).

Beauty is the moment of transition, as if the form were just ready to flow into other forms.

"Beauty," *The Conduct of Life* (1860).

In the true mythology, Love is an immortal child, and Beauty leads him as a guide: nor can we express a deeper sense than when we say, Beauty is the pilot of the young soul.

"Beauty," *The Conduct of Life* (1860).

See also LOVE

It is the most enduring quality, and the most ascending quality.

"Beauty," *The Conduct of Life* (1860).

While thus to love he gave his days
In loyal worship, scorning praise,
How spread their lures for him, in vain,
Thieving Ambition and paltering Gain!
He thought it happier to be dead,
To die for Beauty, than live for bread.

"Beauty," *The Conduct of Life* (1860).

See also AMBITION

Personal beauty is then first charming and itself, when it dissatisfies us with any end; when it becomes a story without an end; when it suggests gleams and visions, and not earthly satisfactions; when it makes the beholder feel his unworthiness; when he cannot feel his right to it, though he were Caesar; he cannot feel more right to it than to the firmament and the splendors of a sunset.

"Love," *Essays*, First Series (1841, repr. 1847).

Beauty is the mark God sets upon virtue.

Nature, ch. 3, (1836, revised and repr. 1849).

See also GOD

Rhodora! if the sages ask thee why
This charm is wasted on the earth and sky,
tell them, dear, that if eyes were made for seeing,
then beauty is its own excuse for being.

"The Rhodora: on Being Asked, Whence Is the Flower?" *Poems* (1847).

We call the beautiful the highest, because it appears to us the golden mean, escaping the dowdiness of the good and the heartlessness of the true.

"The Transcendentalist," repr. in *The Portable Emerson*, ed. Carl Bode (1946, repr. 1981).

Speech, January 1842, at the Masonic Temple in Boston, repr. in *The Dial* (1843) and *Nature, Addresses, and Lectures* (1849).

BEHAVIOR

Mankind divides itself into two classes,—benefactors and malefactors. The second class is vast, the first a handful.

"Considerations by the Way," *The Conduct of Life* (1860).

BELIEF

A deep man believes in miracles, waits for them, believes in magic, believes that the orator will decompose his adversary; believes that the evil eye can wither, that the heart's blessing can heal; that love can exalt talent; can overcome all odds.

"Beauty," *The Conduct of Life* (1860).

So in accepting the leading of the sentiments, it is not what we believe concerning the immortality of the soul, or the like, but *the universal impulse to believe,* that is the material circumstance, and is the principal fact in this history of the globe.

"Experience," *Essays,* Second Series (1844).

See also FAITH

Boasting

It is a capital blunder; as you discover, when another man recites his charities.

"Heroism," *Essays,* First Series (1841, repr. 1847).

See also CHARITY

Body

Wise men read very sharply all your private history in your look and gait and behavior. The whole economy of nature is bent on expression. The tell-tale body is all tongues. Men are like Geneva watches with crystal faces which expose the whole movement.

"Behavior," *The Conduct of Life* (1860).

See also BEHAVIOR

Books

Be a little careful of your Library. Do you foresee what you will do with it? Very little to be sure. But the real question is, What it will do with you? You will come here & get books that will open your eyes, & your ears, & your curiosity, & turn you inside out or outside in.

Emerson in His Journals , ed. by Joel Porte (1982).

Journal entry, July 1873.

Books are for the scholar's idle times. When he can read God directly, the hour is too precious to be wasted in other men's transcripts of their readings.

"The American Scholar," repr. in *Emerson: Essays and Lectures*, ed. Joel Porte (1983).

Oration, August 31, 1837, delivered before the Phi Beta Kappa Society, Cambridge, Massachusetts.

See also INTELLECTUALS

Books are the best things, well used; abused, among the worst. What is the right use? What is the one end, which all means go to effect? They are for nothing but to inspire. I had better never see a book, than to be warped by its attraction clean out of my own orbit, and made a satellite instead of a system.

"The American Scholar," repr. in *Emerson: Essays and Lectures*, ed. Joel Porte (1983).

Oration, August 31, 1837, delivered before the Phi Beta Kappa Society, Cambridge, Massachusetts.

Each age, it is found, must write its own books; or rather, each generation for the next succeeding.

"The American Scholar," repr. in *Emerson: Essays and Lectures*, ed. Joel Porte (1983).

Oration, August 31, 1837, delivered before the Phi Beta Kappa Society, Cambridge, Massachusetts.

Our books approach very slowly the things we most wish to know.

"Beauty," *The Conduct of Life* (1860).

See also KNOWLEDGE

The modernness of all good books seems to give men an existence as wide as man.

"Nominalist and Realist," *Essays*, Second Series (1844).

An imaginative book renders us much more service at first, by stimulating us through its tropes, than afterward, when we arrive at the precise sense of the author. I think nothing is of any value in books, excepting the transcendental and extraordinary.

"The Poet," *Essays*, Second Series (1844).

See also READING

My book should smell of pines and resound with the hum of insects.

"Self-Reliance," *Essays*, First Series (1841, repr. 1847).

See also WRITERS AND WRITING

It is with a good book as it is with good company.

"Spiritual Laws," *Essays*, First Series (1841, repr. 1847).

See also READING

Boys

We teach boys to be such men as we are. We do not teach them to aspire to be all they can. We do not give them a training as if we believed in their noble nature. We scarce educate their bodies. We do not train the eye and the hand. We exercise their understandings to the apprehension and comparison of some facts, to a skill in numbers, in words; we aim to make accountants, attorneys, engineers; but not to make able, earnest, great-hearted men.

"Education," *Lectures and Biographical Sketches* (1883, repr. 1904).

See also EDUCATION

The nonchalance of boys who are sure of a dinner, and would disdain as much as a lord to do or say aught to conciliate one, is the healthy attitude of human nature. A boy is in the parlor what the pit is in the playhouse; independent; irresponsible; looking out from his corner on such people and facts as pass by, he tries and sentences them on their merits, in the swift, summary way of boys, as good, bad, interesting, silly, eloquent, troublesome. He cumbers himself never about consequences, about interests: he gives an independent, genuine verdict.

"Self-Reliance," *Essays*, First Series (1841, repr. 1847).

Budgets

For splendor, there must somewhere be rigid economy. That the head of the house may go brave, the members must be plainly clad, and the town must save that the State may spend.

"Historical Discourse at Concord," *Miscellanies* (1883, repr. 1904).

Speech, September 12, 1835, on the occasion of the second centennial anniversary of the town of Concord.

See also GOVERNMENT

$\mathcal{B}$USINESS AND COMMERCE

The customer is the immediate jewel of our souls. Him we flatter, him we feast, compliment, vote for, and will not contradict.

"Address Delivered in Concord on the Anniversary of the Emancipation of the Negroes in the British West Indies, August 1, 1844," *Miscellanies* (1883, repr. 1904).

See also UNITED STATES

A man should not be a silkworm; nor a nation a tent of caterpillars.

"Wealth," *English Traits* (1856).

The basis of political economy is non-interference. The only safe rule is found in the self-adjusting meter of demand and supply. Do not legislate. Meddle, and you snap the sinews with your sumptuary laws.

"Wealth," *The Conduct of Life* (1860).

The best political economy is the care and culture of men; for, in these crises, all are ruined except such as are proper individuals, capable of thought, and of new choice and the application of their talent to new labor.

"Wealth," *English Traits* (1856).

The crises Emerson refers to here are the cyclical depressions and recessions inherent in the capitalist system. He is specifically referring to the advent of new technologies and raw materials that supersede and then destroy existing industries and products, robbing workers of their jobs and, as Emerson puts it, sacrificing whole towns "like ant hills."

They should own who can administer, not they who hoard and conceal; not they who, the greater proprietors they are, are only the greater beggars, but they whose work carves out work for more, opens a path for all.

"Wealth," *The Conduct of Life* (1860).

$\mathcal{C}$AREERS

A sturdy lad from New Hampshire or Vermont who in turn tries all the professions, who *teams it, farms it, peddles,* keeps a school, preaches, edits a newspaper, goes to Congress, buys a township, and so forth, in successive years, and always, like a cat, falls on his feet, is worth a hundred of these city dolls. He walks abreast with his days and feels no shame in not "studying a profession," for he does not postpone his life, but lives already.

"Self-Reliance," *Essays*, First Series (1841, repr. 1847).

The common experience is, that the man fits himself as well as he can to the customary details of that work or trade he falls into, and tends it as a dog turns a spit. Then he is part of the machine he moves; the man is lost.

"Spiritual Laws," *Essays*, First Series (1841, repr. 1847).

See also WORK

CATHEDRALS

A Gothic cathedral affirms that it was done by us and not done by us.

"History," *Essays*, First Series (1841, repr. 1847).

The Gothic cathedral is a blossoming in stone subdued by the insatiable demand of harmony in man.

"History," *Essays*, First Series (1841, repr. 1847).

CHANGE

There are no fixtures in nature. The universe is fluid and volatile. Permanence is but a word of degrees. Our globe seen by God is a transparent law, not a mass of facts. The law dissolves the fact and holds it fluid.

"Circles," *Essays*, First Series (1841, repr. 1847).

See also FACTS

The lords of life, the lords of life,—
I saw them pass,
In their own guise,
Like and unlike,
Portly and grim,
Use and Surprise,

Surface and Dream,
Succession swift, and spectral Wrong.

"Experience," *Essays*, Second Series (1844).

See also LIFE

The secret of the illusoriness is in the necessity of a succession of moods or objects. Gladly we would anchor, but the anchorage is quicksand.

"Experience," *Essays*, Second Series (1844).

See also PERCEPTION

CHARACTER

Character is higher than intellect. Thinking is the function. Living is the functionary. The stream retreats to its source. A great soul will be strong to live, as well as strong to think.

"The American Scholar," repr. in *Emerson: Essays and Lectures*, ed. Joel Porte (1983).

Oration, August 31, 1837, delivered before the Phi Beta Kappa Society, Cambridge, Massachusetts.

See also ACTION

Character wants room; must not be crowded on by persons, nor be judged from glimpses got in the press of affairs, or on few occasions. It needs perspective, as a great building.

"Character," *Essays*, Second Series (1844).

This is that which we call Character,—a reserved force which acts directly by presence, and without means.

"Character," *Essays*, Second Series (1844).

And the glory of character is in affronting the horrors of depravity to draw thence new nobilities of power: as Art lives and thrills in new use and combining of contrasts, and mining into the dark evermore for blacker pits of night.

"Considerations by the Way," *The Conduct of Life* (1860).

Heaven sometimes hedges a rare character about with ungainliness and odium, as the burr that protects the fruit.

"Culture," *The Conduct of Life* (1860).

For all our penny-wisdom, for all our soul-destroying slavery to habit, it is not to be doubted that all men have sublime thoughts; that all men value the few real hours of life; they love to be heard; they love to be caught up into the vision of principles. We mark with light in the memory the few interviews we have had, in the dreary years of routine and of sin, with souls that made our souls wiser; that spoke what we thought; that told us what we knew; that gave us leave to be what we only were.

"The Divinity School Address," repr. in *The Portable Emerson*, Carl Bode (1946, repr. 1981).

Address, July 15, 1838, delivered before the senior class in Divinity College, Cambridge.

See also INFLUENCES

A man's fortunes are the fruit of his character. A man's friends are his magnetisms.

"Fate," *The Conduct of Life* (1860).

See also FATE

Every man's nature is a sufficient advertisement to him of the character of his fellows.

"Politics," *Essays*, Second Series (1844).

Character teaches above our wills.

"Self-Reliance," *Essays*, First Series (1841, repr. 1847).

That only which we have within, can we see without. If we meet no gods, it is because we harbor none. If there is grandeur in you, you will find grandeur in porters and sweeps. He only is rightly immortal, to whom all things are immortal.

"Worship," *The Conduct of Life* (1860).

CHARITY

We know who is benevolent, by quite other means than the amount of subscriptions to soup-societies. It is only low merits that can be enumerated.

"Character," *Essays*, Second Series (1844).

The worst of charity is, that the lives you are asked to preserve are not worth preserving.

"Considerations by the Way," *The Conduct of Life* (1860).

Then again, do not tell me, as a good man did to-day, of my obligation to put all poor men in good situations. Are they *my* poor? I tell thee, thou foolish philanthropist, that I grudge the dollar, the dime, the cent I give to such men as do not belong to me and to whom I do not belong. There is a class of persons to whom by all spiritual affinity I am bought and sold; for them I will go to prison if need be; but your miscellaneous popular charities; the education at college of fools; the building of meetinghouses to the vain end to which many now stand; alms to sots, and the thousand-fold Relief Societies;—though I confess with shame I sometimes succumb and give the dollar, it is a wicked dollar, which by and by I shall have the manhood to withhold.

"Self-Reliance," *Essays*, First Series (1841, repr. 1847).

This is one in a series of seemingly heartless passages that hearken back to certain difficult sayings of Jesus. See for instance *Matthew* 26:11 where Jesus says: "For you always have the poor with you, but you will not always have me."

Love should make joy; but our benevolence is unhappy. Our Sunday-schools, and churches, and pauper-societies are yokes to the neck. We pain ourselves to please nobody.

"Spiritual Laws," *Essays*, First Series (1841, repr. 1847).

Why should all virtue work in one and the same way? Why should all give dollars? It is very inconvenient to us country folk, and we do not think any good will come of it. We have not dollars; merchants have; let them give them. Farmers will give corn; poets will sing; women will sew; laborers will lend a hand; the children will bring flowers.

"Spiritual Laws," *Essays*, First Series (1841, repr. 1847).

CHRISTIANITY AND CHRISTIANS

We can never see Christianity from the catechism:—from the pastures, from a boat in the pond, from amidst the songs of wood-birds we possibly may.

"Circles," *Essays*, First Series (1841, repr. 1847).

The light struggled in through windows of oiled paper, but they read the word of God by it.

"Historical Discourse at Concord," *Miscellanies* (1883, repr. 1903).

This is a poignant Emersonian image of pure and pious spirituality. Speech, September 12, 1835, on the occasion of the second centennial anniversary of the town of Concord.

See also SPIRITUALITY/PRAYER

I am not engaged to Christianity by decent forms, or saving ordinances; it is not usage, it is not what I do not understand, that binds me to it—let these be the sandy foundations of falsehoods. What I revere and obey in it is its reality, its boundless charity, its deep interior life, the rest it gives to my mind, the echo it returns to my thoughts, the perfect accord it makes with my reason through all its representation of God and His Providence; and the persuasion and courage that come out thence to lead me upward and onward.

"The Lord's Supper," *Miscellanies* (1883, repr. 1904).

Sermon, September 9, 1832, at Second Church, Boston, Massachusetts.

That for which Paul lived and died so gloriously; that for which Jesus gave himself to be crucified; the end that animated the thousand martyrs and heroes who have followed his steps, was to redeem us from a formal religion, and teach us to seek our well-being in the formation of the soul.

"The Lord's Supper," *Miscellanies* (1883, repr. 1904).

Sermon, September 9, 1832, at the Second Church, Boston, Massachusetts.

See also SOUL

CHURCHES

If I should go out of church whenever I hear a false statement I could never stay there five minutes. But why come out? The street is as false as the church, and when I get to my house, or to my manners, or to my speech, I have not got away from the lie.

"New England Reformers," *Essays,* Second Series (1844).

Lecture, March 3, 1844, in Amory Hall, Boston, Massachusetts.

See also SOCIETY

I like the silent church before the service begins, better than any preaching. How far off, how cool, how chaste the persons look, begirt each one with a precinct or sanctuary!

"Self-Reliance," *Essays,* First Series (1841, repr. 1847).

CITIES AND CITY LIFE

New York is a sucked orange. All conversation is at an end, when we have discharged ourselves of a dozen personalities, domestic or imported, which make up our American existence.

"Culture," *The Conduct of Life* (1860).

In our large cities, the population is godless, materialized,—no bond, no fellow-feeling, no enthusiasm. These are not men, but hungers, thirsts, fevers, and appetites walking. How is it people manage to live on,—so aimless as they are? After their peppercorn aims are gained, it seems as if the lime in their bones alone held them together, and not any worthy purpose.

"Worship," *The Conduct of Life* (1860).

COMMON PEOPLE

The literature of the poor, the feelings of the child, the philosophy of the street, the meaning of household life, are the topics of the time. It is a great stride. It is a sign,—is it not? of new vigor, when the extremities are made active, when currents of warm life run into the hands and the feet.

"The American Scholar," repr. in *Emerson: Essays and Lectures,* ed. Joel Porte (1983).

Here Emerson celebrates the fact that writers were beginning to write about common, everyday life. In this way, we can understand Whitman's affinity with Emerson.

See also LITERATURE

If government knew how, I should like to see it check, not multiply the population.

"Considerations by the Way," *The Conduct of Life* (1860).

See also GOVERNMENT

Masses are rude, lame, unmade, pernicious in their demands and influence, and need not to be flattered but to be schooled.

"Considerations by the Way," *The Conduct of Life* (1860).

Shall we then judge a country by the majority, or by the minority? By the minority, surely.

"Considerations by the Way," *The Conduct of Life* (1860).

The mass are animal, in pupilage, and near chimpanzee.

"Considerations by the Way," *The Conduct of Life* (1860).

To say then, the majority are wicked, means no malice, no bad heart in the observer, but, simply that the majority are unripe, and have not yet come to themselves, do not yet know their opinion.

"Considerations by the Way," *The Conduct of Life* (1860).

I am ashamed to see what a shallow village tale our so-called History is. How many times must we say Rome, and Paris, and Constantinople! What does Rome know of rat and lizard? What are Olympiads and Consulates to these neighboring systems of being? Nay, what food or experience or succor have they for the Esquimaux seal-hunter, or the Kanaka in his canoe, for the fisherman, the stevedore, the porter?

"History," *Essays*, First Series (1841, repr. 1847).

The idiot, the Indian, the child and unschooled farmer's boy, stand nearer to the light by which nature is to be read, than the dissector or the antiquary.

"History," *Essays*, First Series (1841, repr. 1847).

When private men shall act with original views, the lustre will be transferred from the actions of kings to those of gentlemen.

"Self-Reliance," *Essays*, First Series (1841, repr. 1847).

COMMUNITIES

All are needed by each one;
Nothing is fair or good alone.

"Each and All," *Poems* (1847).

See also SOLITUDE

COMPANY

In good company, the individuals merge their egotism into a social soul exactly co-extensive with the several consciousnesses there present.

"Friendship," *Essays*, First Series (1841, repr. 1847).

A man should not go where he cannot carry his whole sphere or society with him,—not bodily, the whole circle of his friends, but atmospherically. He should preserve in a new company the same attitude of mind and reality of relation, which his daily associates draw him to, else he is shorn of his best beams, and will be an orphan in the merriest club.

"Manners," *Essays*, Second Series (1844).

I like that every chair should be a throne, and hold a king.

"Manners," *Essays*, Second Series (1844).

We should meet each morning, as from foreign countries, and spending the day together, should depart at night, as into foreign countries.

"Manners," *Essays*, Second Series (1844).

We are imprisoned in life in the company of persons powerfully unlike us.

Quoted in Robert D. Richardson, Jr., *Emerson: The Mind on Fire*, ch. 31, (1995).

Journal entry, January, 1845.

See also ALIENATION

There is a mortifying experience in particular, which does not fail to wreak itself also in the general history; I mean "the foolish face of praise," the forced smile which we put on in company where we do not feel at ease, in answer to conversation which does not interest us. The muscles, not spontaneously moved but moved, by a low usurping wilfulness, grow tight about the outline of the face, with the most disagreeable sensation.

"Self-Reliance," *Essays*, First Series (1841, repr. 1847).

See also CONVERSATION

Confidence

We are such lovers of self-reliance, that we excuse in a man many sins, if he will show us a complete satisfaction in his position, which asks no leave to be, of mine, or any man's good opinion.

"Manners," *Essays*, Second Series (1844).

Insist on yourself; never imitate.

"Self-Reliance," *Essays*, First Series (1841, repr. 1847).

See also SELF

The power men possess to annoy me I give them by a weak curiosity. No man can come near me but through my act.

"Self-Reliance," *Essays*, First Series (1841, repr. 1847).

Conflict

Nature is upheld by antagonism.

"Considerations by the Way," *The Conduct of Life* (1860).

Though your views are in straight antagonism to theirs, assume an identity of sentiment, assume that you are saying precisely that which all think, and in the flow of wit and love roll out your paradoxes in solid column, with not the infirmity of a doubt.

"Prudence," *Essays*, First Series (1841, repr. 1847).

CONFORMITY

Men in history, men in the world of to-day are bugs, are spawn, and are called "the mass" and "the herd."

"The American Scholar," repr. in *Emerson: Essays and Lectures*, ed. Joel Porte (1983).

Nietzsche was greatly influenced by Emerson's writings and we can hear a definite Nietszchean ring in this sentence.

Adhere to your own act, and congratulate yourself if you have done something strange and extravagant, and broken the monotony of a decorous age.

"Heroism," *Essays*, First Series (1841, repr. 1847).

I hope in these days we have heard the last of conformity and consistency. Let the words be gazetted and ridiculous henceforward. Instead of the gong for dinner, let us hear a whistle from the Spartan fife.

"Self-Reliance," *Essays*, First Series (1841, repr. 1847).

Well, most men have bound their eyes with one or another handkerchief, and attached themselves to some of these communities of opinion. This conformity makes them not false in a few particulars, authors of a few lies, but false in all particulars. Their every truth is not quite true. Their two is not the real two, their four not the real four; so that every word they say chagrins us and we know not where to set them right.

"Self-Reliance," *Essays*, First Series (1841, repr. 1847).

See also TRUTH

Whoso would be a man, must be a nonconformist.

"Self-Reliance," *Essays*, First Series (1841, repr. 1847).

CONNECTEDNESS

The near explains the far. The drop is a small ocean. A man is related to all nature. This perception of the worth of the vulgar is fruitful in discoveries. Goethe, in this very thing the most modern of the moderns, has shown us, as none ever did, the genius of the ancients.

"The American Scholar," repr. in *Emerson: Essays and Lectures*, ed. Joel Porte (1983).

Oration, August 31, 1837, delivered before the Phi Beta Kappa Society, Cambridge, Massachusetts.

I cannot spare water or wine,
 Tobacco-leaf, or poppy, or rose;
From the earth-poles to the line,
 All between that works or grows,
Every thing is kin of mine.

"Mithridates," *Poems* (1847).

See also NATURE

The inmost in due time becomes the outmost.

"Self-Reliance," *Essays*, First Series (1841, repr. 1847).

See also SELF

Consciousness

It is very unhappy, but too late to be helped, the discovery we have made, that we exist. That discovery is called the Fall of Man. Ever afterwards, we suspect our instruments.

"Experience," *Essays*, Second Series (1844).

See also SKEPTICISM

The consciousness in each man is a sliding scale, which identifies him now with the First Cause, and now with the flesh of his body; life above life, in infinite degrees.

"Experience," *Essays*, Second Series (1844).

See also SPIRITUALITY/PRAYER

One key, one solution to the mysteries of the human condition, one solution to the old knots of fate, freedom, and foreknowledge, exists, the propounding, namely, of the double consciousness. A man must ride alternately on the horses of his private and public nature, as the equestrians in the circus throw themselves nimbly from horse to horse, or plant one foot on the back of one, and the other foot on the back of the other.

"Fate," *The Conduct of Life* (1860).

CONSERVATIVES

All conservatives are such from personal defects. They have been effeminated by position or nature, born halt and blind, through luxury of their parents, and can only, like invalids, act on the defensive. But strong natures, backwoodsmen, New Hampshire giants, Napoleons, Burkes, Broughams, Websters, Kossuths, are inevitable patriots, until their life ebbs, and their defects and gout, palsy and money, warp them.

"Fate," *The Conduct of Life* (1860).

Men are conservatives when they are least vigorous, or when they are most luxurious. They are conservatives after dinner, or before taking their rest; when they are sick, or aged: in the morning, or when their intellect or their conscience has been aroused, when they hear music, or when they read poetry, they are radicals.

"New England Reformers," *Essays*, Second Series (1844).

Lecture, March 3, 1844, in Amory Hall, Boston, Massachusetts.

On the other side, the conservative party, composed of the most moderate, able, and cultivated part of the population, is timid, and merely defensive of property. It vindicates no right, it aspires to no real good, it brands no crime, it proposes no generous policy, it does not build, nor write, nor cherish the arts, nor foster religion, nor establish schools, nor encourage science, nor emancipate the slave, nor befriend the poor, or the Indian, or the immigrant.

"Politics," *Essays*, Second Series (1844).

See also POLITICS

Conservatism, ever more timorous and narrow, disgusts the children, and drives them for a mouthful of fresh air into radicalism.

"Power," *The Conduct of Life* (1860).

Consistency

But when you have chosen your part, abide by it, and do not weakly try to reconcile yourself with the world.

"Heroism," *Essays*, First Series (1841, repr. 1847).

Unless, of course, "your part" turns out to be a "foolish consistency."

A foolish consistency is the hobgoblin of little minds, adored by little statesmen and philosophers and divines.

"Self-Reliance," *Essays*, First Series (1841, repr. 1847).

See also CONFORMITY

Conversation

I know nothing which life has to offer so satisfying as the profound good understanding, which can subsist, after much exchange of good offices, between two virtuous men, each of whom is sure of himself, and sure of his friend. It is a happiness which postpones all other gratifications, and makes politics, and commerce, and churches, cheap.

"Character," *Essays*, Second Series (1844).

See also FRIENDS AND FRIENDSHIP

Good as is discourse, silence is better, and shames it.

"Circles," *Essays*, First Series (1847).

See also SILENCE

Conversation is an art in which a man has all mankind for his competitors, for it is that which all are practising every day while they live.

"Considerations by the Way," *The Conduct of Life* (1860).

Truly speaking, it is not instruction, but provocation, that I can receive from another soul. What he announces, I must find true in me, or reject; and on his word, or as his second, be he who he may, I can accept nothing.

"The Divinity School Address," repr. in *The Portable Emerson*, ed. Carl Bode (1946, repr. 1981).

Address, July 15, 1838, delivered before the senior class in Divinity College, Cambridge.

See also INDIVIDUALISM

Great conversation . . . requires an absolute running of two souls into one.

"Friendship," *Essays*, First Series (1841, repr. 1847).

What a perpetual disappointment is actual society, even of the virtuous and gifted! After interviews have been compassed with long foresight, we must be tormented presently by baffled blows, by sudden, unseasonable apathies, by epilepsies of wit and of animal spirits, in the heyday of friendship and thought. Our faculties do not play us true, and both parties are relieved by solitude.

"Friendship," *Essays*, First Series (1841, repr. 1847).

See also FRIENDS AND FRIENDSHIP

In all things I would have the island of a man inviolate. Let us sit apart as the gods, talking from peak to peak all round Olympus. No degree of affection need invade this religion.

"Manners," *Essays*, Second Series (1844).

The love of beauty is mainly the love of measure or proportion. The person who screams, or uses the superlative degree, or converses with heat, puts whole drawing-rooms to flight.

"Manners," *Essays*, Second Series (1844).

See also COMPANY

In all conversation between two persons, tacit reference is made, as to a third party, to a common nature. That third party or common nature is not social; it is impersonal; is God.

"The Over-Soul," *Essays*, First Series (1841, repr. 1847).

Emerson's notion of conversation has been taken to be akin to his idea of conversion.

See also GOD

Conversion

To aim to convert a man by miracles is a profanation of the soul. A true conversion, a true Christ, is now, as always, to be made by the reception of beautiful sentiments.

"The Divinity School Address," repr. in *The Portable Emerson*, ed. Carl Bode (1946, repr. 1981).

Address, July 15, 1838, delivered before the senior class in Divinity College, Cambridge.

See also CHRISTIANITY AND CHRISTIANS

Conviction

The measure of a master is his success in bringing all men round to his opinion twenty years later.

"Culture," *The Conduct of Life* (1860).

See also LEADERSHIP

Courage

A great part of courage is the courage of having done the thing before.

"Culture," *The Conduct of Life* (1860).

There is always safety in valor.

"The Times," *English Traits* (1856).

Cowardice

God will not make himself manifest to cowards.

"The Over-Soul," *Essays*, First Series (1841, repr. 1847).

See also GOD

Creation, the

The dice of God are always loaded. The world looks like a multiplication-table, or a mathematical equation, which, turn it how you will, balances itself.

"Compensation," *Essays*, First Series (1841, repr. 1847).

See also GOD

The world globes itself in a drop of dew.

"Compensation," *Essays*, First Series (1841, repr. 1847).

Each particle is a microcosm, and faithfully renders the likeness of the world.

Nature, ch. 5, (1836, revised and repr. 1849).

Philosophically considered, the universe is composed of Nature and the Soul.

Nature, Introduction, (1836, revised and repr. 1849).

Emerson goes on to explain that by "nature" he means everything that is "not me," hence not only the trees and the sun and the moon, but other people, art, as well as one's own body. This formulation with its Cartesian echoes becomes articulated in more acrimonious (and ironic) terms in the essay "Self-Reliance," when Emerson writes: "Man is timid and apologetic; he is no longer upright; he dares not say 'I think,' 'I am,' but quotes some saint or sage." The saint or sage is, of course, Descartes.

See also SOUL

The world proceeds from the same spirit as the body of man. It is a remoter and inferior incarnation of God, a projection of God in the unconscious.

Nature, ch. 7, (1836, revised and repr. 1849).

See also NATURE

What angels invented these splendid ornaments, these rich conveniences, this ocean of air above, this ocean of water beneath, this firmament of earth between? this zodiac of lights, this tent of dropping clouds, this striped coat of climates, this fourfold year?

Nature, ch. 2, (1836, revised and repr. 1849).

See also NATURE

For the world is not painted, or adorned, but is from the beginning beautiful; and God has not made some beautiful things, but Beauty is the creator of the universe.

"The Poet," *Essays*, Second Series (1844).

See also BEAUTY

The eye repeats every day the first eulogy on things—"He saw that they were good."

"Uses of Great Men," *Representative Men* (1850).

See also EYES

God hid the whole world in thy heart.

"Woodnotes II," *Poems* (1847).

CREATIVITY

Because the soul is progressive, it never quite repeats itself, but in every act attempts the production of a new and fairer whole.

"Art," *Essays,* First Series (1841, repr. 1847).

But it is impossible that the creative power should exclude itself. Into every intelligence there is a door which is never closed, through which the creator passes.

"Experience," *Essays,* Second Series (1844).

For all men live by truth, and stand in need of expression. In love, in art, in avarice, in politics, in labor, in games, we study to utter our painful secret. The man is only half himself, the other half is his expression.

"The Poet," *Essays,* Second Series (1844).

See also TRUTH

Through man, and woman, and sea, and star,
Saw the dance of nature forward far;
Through worlds, and races, and terms, and times,
Saw musical order, and pairing rhymes.

"The Poet," *Essays,* Second Series (1844).

See also ART AND ARTISTS

CRIME

Commit a crime and the world is made of glass. Commit a crime, and it seems as if a coat of snow fell on the ground, such as reveals in the woods the track of every partridge and fox and squirrel and mole.

"Compensation," *Essays,* First Series (1841, repr. 1847).

The reason of idleness and of crime is the deferring of our hopes. Whilst we are waiting, we beguile the time with jokes, with sleep, with eating, and with crimes.

"Nominalist and Realist," *Essays*, Second Series (1844).

CRITICISM

Good criticism is very rare and always precious.

"Culture," *The Conduct of Life* (1860).

It is true that the discerning intellect of the world is always much in advance of the creative, so that there are competent judges of the best book, and few writers of the best books.

"Intellect," *Essays*, First Series (1841, repr. 1847).

See also BOOKS

If you criticize a fine genius, the odds are that you are out of your reckoning, and, instead of the poet, are censuring your own caricature of him.

"Nominalist and Realist," *Essays*, Second Series (1844).

Criticism is infested with the cant of materialism, which assumes that manual skill and activity is the first merit of all men, and disparages such as say and do not, overlooking the fact, that some men, namely, poets, are natural sayers, sent into the world to the end of expression, and confounds them with those whose province is action, but who quit to imitate the sayers.

"The Poet," *Essays*, Second Series (1844).

See also POETRY AND POETS

Those who are esteemed umpires of taste, are often persons who have acquired some knowledge of admired pictures or sculptures, and have an inclination for whatever is elegant; but if you inquire whether they are beautiful souls, and whether their own acts are like fair pictures, you learn that they are selfish and sensual. Their cultivation is local, as if you should rub a log of dry wood in one spot to produce fire, all the rest remaining cold.

"The Poet," *Essays*, Second Series (1844).

CULTURE

Not out of those, on whom systems of education have exhausted their culture, comes the helpful giant to destroy the old or to build the new, but out of unhandselled savage nature, out of terrible Druids and Berserkirs, come at last Alfred and Shakespeare.

"The American Scholar," repr. in *Emerson: Essays and Lectures*, ed. Joel Porte (1983).

Oration, August 31, 1837, delivered before the Phi Beta Kappa Society, Cambridge, Massachusetts.

The time will come when the evil forms we have known can no more be organized. Man's culture can spare nothing, wants all material. He is to convert all impediments into instruments, all enemies into power.

"Culture," *The Conduct of Life* (1860).

DEATH

The death of a dear friend, wife, brother, lover, which seemed nothing but privation, somewhat later assumes the aspect of a guide or genius; for it commonly operates revolutions in our way of life, terminates an epoch of infancy or of youth which was waiting to be closed, breaks up a wonted occupation, or a household, or style of living, and allows for the formation of new ones more friendly to the growth of character.

"Compensation," *Essays*, First Series (1841, repr. 1847).

In the death of my son, now more than two years ago, I seem to have lost a beautiful estate,—no more. I cannot get it nearer to me.

"Experience," *Essays*, Second Series (1844).

The dearest events are summer-rain, and we the Para coats that shed every drop. Nothing is left us now but death. We look to that with grim satisfaction, saying, there at least is reality that will not dodge us.

"Experience," *Essays*, Second Series (1844).

See also EXPERIENCE

Nothing is dead: men feign themselves dead, and endure mock funerals and mournful obituaries, and there they stand looking out of the window, sound and well, in some new and strange disguise.

"Nominalist and Realist," *Essays*, Second Series (1844).

Every thing admonishes us how needlessly long life is.

"The Transcendentalist," repr. in *The Portable Emerson*, ed. Carl Bode (1946, repr. 1981).

Speech, January 1842, at the Masonic Temple in Boston, repr. in *The Dial* (1843) and *Nature, Addresses, and Lectures* (1849).

See also LIFE

DEBT

You must pay at last your own debt. If you are wise, you will dread a prosperity which only loads you with more.

"Compensation," *Essays*, First Series (1841, repr. 1847).

Debt, grinding debt, whose iron face the widow, the orphan, and the sons of genius fear and hate;—debt, which consumes so much time, which so cripples and disheartens a great spirit with cares that seem so base, is a preceptor whose lessons cannot be forgone, and is needed most by those who suffer from it most.

Nature, ch. 5, (1836, revised and repr. 1849).

DEPENDENCE

We do not quite forgive a giver. The hand that feeds us is in some danger of being bitten. We can receive anything from love, for that is a way of receiving it from ourselves; but not from any one who assumes to bestow. We sometimes hate the meat which we eat, because there seems something of degrading dependence in living it.

"Gifts," *Essays*, Second Series (1844).

See also GIFTS

DISSATISFACTION

There are three wants which can never be satisfied: that of the rich, who wants something more; that of the sick, who wants something different; and that of the traveller, who says, "Anywhere but here."

"Considerations by the Way," *The Conduct of Life* (1860).

Want is a growing giant whom the coat of Have was never large enough to cover.

"Wealth," *The Conduct of Life* (1860).

DRUGS

"A man," said Oliver Cromwell, "never rises so high as when he knows not whither he is going." Dreams and drunkenness, the use of opium and alcohol are the semblance and counterfeit of this oracular genius, and hence their dangerous attraction for men. For the like reason they ask the aid of wild passions, as in gaming and war, to ape in some manner these flames and generosities of the heart.

"Circles," Essays, First Series (1841, repr. 1847).

See also GENIUS

The spirit of the world, the great calm presence of the creator, comes not forth to the sorceries of opium or of wine. The sublime vision comes to the pure and simple soul in a clean and chaste body.

"The Poet," Essays, Second Series (1844).

EARTH

Earth's a howling wilderness,
Truculent with fraud and force.

"Berrying," *Poems* (1847).

The poem is an argument against this idea.

See also SUFFERING

Mine and yours;
Mine, not yours.
Earth endures.

"Hamatreya," *Poems* (1847).

The rounded world is fair to see,
Nine times folded in mystery.

"Nature," *Essays*, Second Series (1844).

*E*DUCATION

Give a boy address and accomplishments and you give him the mastery of palaces and fortunes where he goes.

"Behavior," *The Conduct of Life* (1860).

A man of sense and energy, the late head of the Farm School in Boston Harbor, said to me, "I want none of your good boys,—give me the bad ones." And this is the reason, I suppose, why, as soon as the children are good, the mothers are scared, and think they are going to die.

"Considerations by the Way," *The Conduct of Life* (1860).

See also BOYS

We shall one day learn to supersede politics by education. What we call our root-and-branch reforms of slavery, war, gambling, intemperance, is only medicating the symptoms. We must begin higher up, namely, in Education.

"Culture," *The Conduct of Life* (1860).

You send your child to the schoolmaster, but 'tis the schoolboys who educate him. You send him to the Latin class, but much of his tuition comes, on his way to school, from the shop-windows.

"Culture," *The Conduct of Life* (1860).

The great object of Education should be commensurate with the object of life. It should be a moral one; to teach self-trust: to inspire the youthful man with an interest in himself; with a curiosity touching his own nature; to acquaint him with the resources of his mind, and to teach him that there is all his strength, and to inflame him with a piety towards the

Grand Mind in which he lives. Thus would education conspire with the Divine Providence.

"Education," *Lectures and Biographical Sketches* (1883, repr. 1904).

We are by nature observers, and thereby learners. That is our permanent state.

"Love," *Essays*, First Series (1841, repr. 1847).

See also MANKIND

But in a hundred high schools and colleges, this warfare against common-sense still goes on. Four, or six, or ten years, the pupil is parsing Greek and Latin, and as soon as he leaves the University, as it is ludicrously called, he shuts those books for the last time. Some thousands of young men are graduated at our colleges in this country every year, and the persons who, at forty years, still read Greek, can all be counted on your hand. I never met with ten. Four or five persons I have seen who read Plato. But is not this absurd, that the whole liberal talent of this country should be directed in its best years on studies which lead to nothing?

"New England Reformers," *Essays*, Second Series (1844).

Lecture, March 3, 1844, in Amory Hall, Boston, Massachusetts.

Men do not believe in the power of education. We do not think we can speak to divine sentiments in man, and we do not try. We renounce all high aims.

"New England Reformers," *Essays*, Second Series (1844).

Lecture, March 3, 1844, in Amory Hall, Boston, Massachusetts.

The Roman rule was, to teach a boy nothing that he could not learn standing. The old English rule was, "All summer in the field, and all winter in the study." And it seems as if a man should learn to plant, or to fish, or to hunt, that he might secure his subsistence at all events, and not be painful to his friends and fellow men.

"New England Reformers," *Essays*, Second Series (1844).

Lecture, March 3, 1844, in Amory Hall, Boston, Massachusetts.

We are students of words: we are shut up in schools, and colleges, and recitation-rooms, for ten or fifteen years, and come out at last with a bag of wind, a memory of words, and do not know a thing.

"New England Reformers," *Essays*, Second Series (1844).

Lecture, March 3, 1844, in Amory Hall, Boston, Massachusetts.

The advantage in education is always with those children who slip up into life without being objects of notice.

Quoted in Robert D. Richardson, Jr., *Emerson: The Mind on Fire*, ch. 4, (1995).

The intellect is vagabond, and our system of education fosters restlessness. Our minds travel when our bodies are forced to stay at home. We imitate; and what is imitation but the travelling of the mind?

"Self-Reliance," *Essays*, First Series (1841, repr. 1847).

What we do not call education is more precious than that which we call so.

"Spiritual Laws," *Essays*, First Series (1841, repr. 1847).

Egotism

The pest of society is egotists. There are dull and bright, sacred and profane, coarse and fine egotists. 'Tis a disease that, like influenza, falls on all constitutions.

"Culture," *The Conduct of Life* (1860).

Emerson, Ralph Waldo

But lest I should mislead any when I have my own head and obey my whims, let me remind the reader that I am only an experimenter. Do not set the least value on what I do, or the least discredit on what I do not, as if I pretended to settle any thing as true or false. I unsettle all things. No facts are to me sacred; none are profane; I simply experiment, an endless seeker with no Past at my back.

"Circles," *Essays*, First Series (1841, repr. 1847).

See also TRUTH

Then, though I prize my friends, I cannot afford to talk with them and study their visions, lest I lose my own. It would indeed give me a certain household joy to quit this lofty seeking, this spiritual astronomy, or search of stars, and come down to warm sympathies with you; but then I know well I shall mourn always the vanishing of my mighty gods.

"Friendship," *Essays*, First Series (1841, repr. 1847).

See also FRIENDS AND FRIENDSHIP

I have been told, that in some public discourses of mine my reverence for the intellect has made me unjustly cold to the personal relations. But now I almost shrink at the remembrance of such disparaging words. For persons are love's world, and the coldest philosopher cannot recount the debt of the young soul wandering here in nature to the power of love, without being tempted to unsay, as treasonable to nature, aught derogatory to the social instincts.

"Love," *Essays*, First Series (1841, repr. 1847).

See also LOVE

For his lips could well pronounce
Words that were persuasions.

"Threnody," *Poems* (1847).

Emerson is lamenting the death of his son Waldo.

ENVY

Every ship is a romantic object, except that we sail in. Embark, and the romance quits our vessel, and hangs on every other sail in the horizon.

"Experience," *Essays*, Second Series (1844).

ETERNITY

Our life is an apprenticeship to the truth, that around every circle another can be drawn; that there is no end in nature, but every end is a beginning; that there is always another dawn risen on mid-noon, and under every deep a lower deep opens.

"Circles," *Essays*, First Series (1841, repr. 1847).

Where do we find ourselves? In a series of which we do not know the extremes, and believe that it has none. We wake and find ourselves on a stair; there are stairs below us, which we seem to have ascended; there are stairs above us, many a one, which go upward and out of sight.

"Experience," *Essays*, Second Series (1844).

See also LIFE

Nothing divine dies. All good is eternally reproductive. The beauty of nature reforms itself in the mind, and not for barren contemplation, but for new creation.

Nature, ch. 3, (1836, revised and repr. 1849).

See also NATURE

It is the secret of the world that all things subsist and do not die, but only retire from sight and afterwards return again.

"Nominalist and Realist," *Essays*, Second Series (1844).

*E*THICS AND MORALITY

The moral sense is always supported by the permanent interest of the parties. Else, I know not how, in our world, any good would ever get done.

"Address Delivered in Concord on the Anniversary of the Emancipation of the Negroes in the British West Indies, August 1, 1844," *Miscellanies* (1883, repr. 1904).

All things are moral. That soul, which within us is a sentiment, outside of us is a law. We feel its inspiration; out there in history we can see its fatal strength.

"Compensation," *Essays*, First Series (1841, repr. 1847).

Let us treat the men and women well: treat them as if they were real: perhaps they are.

"Experience," *Essays*, Second Series (1844).

A sly articulation of Emersonian skepticism.

See also RELATIONSHIPS

Therefore all just persons are satisfied with their own praise. They refuse to explain themselves, and are content that new actions should do them that office. They believe that we communicate without speech, and above speech, and that no right action of ours is quite unaffecting to our friends, at whatever distance; for the influence of action is not to be measured by miles.

"Experience," *Essays,* Second Series (1844).

See also ACTION

And last of all, high over thought, in the world of morals, Fate appears as vindicator, levelling the high, lifting the low, requiring justice in man, and always striking soon or late when justice is not done. What is useful will last, what is hurtful will sink.

"Fate," *The Conduct of Life* (1860).

This is Emerson in a utilitarian mood. He will later catch himself and warn us of overhasty generalizations.

See also FATE

All things are moral; and in their boundless changes have an unceasing reference to spiritual nature.

Nature, ch. 5, (1836, revised and repr. 1849).

See also SPIRITUALITY/PRAYER

Ethics and religion differ herein; that the one is the system of human duties commencing from man; the other, from God. Religion includes the personality of God; Ethics does not.

Nature, ch. 6, (1836, revised and repr. 1849).

See also RELIGION

Good and bad are but names very readily transferable to that or this; the only right is what is after my constitution; the only wrong what is against it.

"Self-Reliance," *Essays,* First Series (1841, repr. 1847).

Truth is handsomer than the affectation of love. Your goodness must have some edge to it,—else it is none.

"Self-Reliance," *Essays,* First Series (1841, repr. 1847).

See also TRUTH

Exaggeration

Exaggeration is in the course of things. Nature sends no creature, no man into the world, without adding a small excess of his proper quality. Given the planet, it is still necessary to add the impulse; so, to every creature nature added a little violence of direction in its proper path, a shove to put it on its way; in every instance, a slight generosity, a drop too much.

"Nature," *Essays*, Second Series (1844).

We aim above the mark, to hit the mark. Every act hath some falsehood of exaggeration in it.

"Nature," *Essays*, Second Series (1844).

There is no one who does not exaggerate. In conversation, men are encumbered with personality, and talk too much.

"Nominalist and Realist," *Essays*, Second Series (1844).

See also CONVERSATION

Experience

The years teach much which the days never know.

"Experience," *Essays*, Second Series (1844).

We thrive by casualties. Our chief experiences have been casual.

"Experience," *Essays*, Second Series (1844).

In the context of the essay, Emerson not only puns on casual and casualty but also on causality.

Everything is beautiful seen from the point of the intellect, or as truth. But all is sour, if seen as experience.

"Love," *Essays*, First Series (1841, repr. 1847).

God! I will not be an owl,
But sun me in the capitol.

"Mithridates," *Poems* (1847).

Emerson sings this after he has resolved to dive into the world of experience, even if he would be killed by too much creation. He therefore will not, as an owl does, watch from afar at night, but will with gusto take on the day. "Capitol" refers to the highest of the seven hills of Rome and to the temple of Jupiter there, but we should not forget the political dimensions of "Capitol" and apply these also to Emerson's ultimate message.

*E*YES

The eyes of men converse as much as their tongues, with the advantage that the ocular dialect needs no dictionary, but is understood all the world over.

"Behavior," *The Conduct of Life* (1860).

See also CONVERSATION

The glance is natural magic. The mysterious communication established across a house between two entire strangers, moves all the springs of wonder. The communication by the glance is in the greatest part not subject to the control of the will. It is the bodily symbol of identity with nature. We look into the eyes to know if this other form is another self, and the eyes will not lie, but make a faithful confession what inhabitant is there.

"Behavior," *The Conduct of Life* (1860).

The 20th-century existentialist philosopher Jean-Paul Sartre also ruminates on the implications for the self of the glance or the stare, but he presents darker aspects of this "communication," as Emerson calls it. For Sartre, another's glance robs the individual of his ability to define his own self. See Sartre's *Being and Nothingness*.

See also SELF

There are eyes, to be sure, that give no more admission into the man than blueberries.

"Behavior," *The Conduct of Life* (1860).

See also PERCEPTION

The eye is the first circle; the horizon which it forms is the second; and throughout nature this primary figure is repeated without end. It is the highest emblem in the cipher of the world.

"Circles," *Essays*, First Series (1841, repr. 1847).

As a rule of thumb, when Emerson talks about the "eye" he is punning on the "I," that is, the self.

See also PERCEPTION

The health of the eye seems to demand a horizon. We are never tired, so long as we can see far enough.

Nature, ch. 3, (1836, revised and repr. 1849).

*F*ACTS

All public facts are to be individualized, all private facts are to be generalized.

"History," *Essays*, First Series (1841, repr. 1847).

A representative maxim indicating that Emerson's notion of individualism was not a form of solipsism, but involved a social component.

See also INDIVIDUALISM

A fact is the end or last issue of spirit. The visible creation is the terminus or the circumference of the invisible world.

Nature, ch. 4, (1836, revised and repr. 1849).

See also KNOWLEDGE

To the wise, therefore, a fact is true poetry, and the most beautiful of fables.

Nature, ch. 8, (1836, revised and repr. 1849).

*F*AITH

Our faith comes in moments; our vice is habitual.

"The Over-Soul," *Essays*, First Series (1841, repr. 1847).

The faith that stands on authority is not faith.

"The Over-Soul," *Essays*, First Series (1841, repr. 1847).

For Nature ever faithful is
To such as trust her faithfulness.
When the forest shall mislead me,
When the night and morning lie,

When the sea and land refuse to feed me,
'Twill be time enough to die.

"Woodnotes I," *Poems* (1847).

See also NATURE

*F*AMILIES

In the country, without any interference from the law, the agricultural life
favors the permanence of families.

"Historical Discourse at Concord," *Miscellanies* (1883, repr. 1904).

Speech given September 12, 1835 on the occasion of the second centennial anniversary of the
town of Concord.

See also FARMS AND FARMING

Why should we assume the faults of our friend, or wife, or father, or child,
because they sit around our hearth, or are said to have the same blood?

"Self-Reliance," *Essays*, First Series (1841, repr. 1847).

*F*ARMS AND FARMING

An orchard, good tillage, good grounds, seem a fixture, like a gold mine,
or a river, to a citizen; but to a large farmer, not much more fixed than the
state of the crop.

"Circles," *Essays*, First Series (1841, repr. 1847).

See also CHANGE

What is a farm but a mute gospel? The chaff and the wheat, weeds and
plants, blight, rain, insects, sun—it is a sacred emblem from the first
furrow of spring to the last stack which the snow of winter overtakes in
the fields.

Nature, ch. 5, (1836, revised and repr. 1849).

*F*AT E

An expense of ends to means is fate;—organization tyrannizing over character. The menagerie, or forms and powers of the spine, is a book of fate: the bill of the bird, the skull of the snake, determines tyrannically its limits.

"Fate," *The Conduct of Life* (1860).

But every jet of chaos which threatens to exterminate us is convertible by intellect into wholesome force. Fate is unpenetrated causes.

"Fate," *The Conduct of Life* (1860).

Fate then is a name for facts not yet passed under the fire of thought;— for causes which are unpenetrated.

"Fate," *The Conduct of Life* (1860).

If you believe in Fate to your harm, believe it, at least, for your good.

"Fate," *The Conduct of Life* (1860).

The element running through entire nature, which we popularly call Fate, is known to us as limitation. Whatever limits us, we call Fate.

"Fate," *The Conduct of Life* (1860).

'Tis weak and vicious people who cast the blame on Fate. The right use of Fate is to bring up our conduct to the loftiness of nature.

"Fate," *The Conduct of Life* (1860).

Every man beholds his human condition with a degree of melancholy. As a ship aground is battered by the waves, so man, imprisoned in mortal life, lies open to the mercy of coming events.

"Intellect," *Essays,* First Series (1841, repr. 1847).

In the most worn, pedantic, introverted self-tormenter's life, the greatest part is incalculable by him, unforeseen, unimaginable, and must be, until he can take himself up by his own ears. What am I? What has my will done to make me that I am? Nothing. I have been floated into this thought, this hour, this connection of events, by secret currents of might and mind, and my ingenuity and wilfulness have not thwarted, have not aided to an appreciable degree.

"Intellect," *Essays*, First Series (1841, repr. 1847).

See also INTELLECTUALS

Things are in the saddle,
And ride mankind.

"Ode Inscribed to W.H. Channing," *Poems* (1847).

Accept the place the divine providence has found for you, the society of your contemporaries, the connection of events.

"Self-Reliance," *Essays*, First Series (1841, repr. 1847).

*F*AULTS AND FAULT-FINDING

Every man in his lifetime needs to thank his faults.

"Compensation," *Essays*, First Series (1841, repr. 1847).

This is so, according to Emerson, because we will then be able to recognize our true talents and be able to understand the successes and failures of other people.

*F*EAR

Fear always springs from ignorance.

"The American Scholar," repr. in *Emerson: Essays and Lectures*, ed. Joel Porte (1983).

Oration, August 31, 1837, delivered before the Phi Beta Kappa Society, Cambridge, Massachusetts.

It was a high counsel that I once heard given to a young person,—"Always do what you are afraid to do."

"Heroism," *Essays*, First Series (1841, repr. 1847).

*F*RIENDS AND FRIENDSHIP

Friendship should be surrounded with ceremonies and respects, and not crushed into corners. Friendship requires more time than poor busy men can usually command.

"Behavior," *The Conduct of Life* (1860).

A man's growth is seen in the successive choirs of his friends. For every friend whom he loses for truth, he gains a better.

"Circles," *Essays*, First Series (1841, repr. 1847).

A day for toil, an hour for sport,
But for a friend is life too short.

"Considerations by the Way," *The Conduct of Life* (1860).

A new person is to me a great event, and hinders me from sleep. I have often had fine fancies about persons which have given me delicious hours; but the joy ends in the day; it yields no fruit.

"Friendship," *Essays*, First Series (1841, repr. 1847).

Almost every man we meet requires some civility,—requires to be humored; he has some fame, some talent, some whim of religion or philanthropy in his head that is not to be questioned, and which spoils all conversation with him. But a friend is a sane man who exercises not my ingenuity, but me.

"Friendship," *Essays*, First Series (1841, repr. 1847).

Friendship demands a religious treatment. We talk of choosing our friends, but friends are self-elected. Reverence is a great part of it.

"Friendship," *Essays*, First Series (1841, repr. 1847).

I awoke this morning with a devout thanksgiving for my friends, the old and the new. Shall I not call God the Beautiful, who daily showeth himself to me in his gifts?

"Friendship," *Essays*, First Series (1841, repr. 1847).

I do then with my friends as I do with my books. I would have them where I can find them, but I seldom use them. We must have society on our own terms, and admit or exclude it on the slightest cause.

"Friendship," *Essays*, First Series (1841, repr. 1847).

See also SOCIETY

I hate the prostitution of the name of friendship to signify modish and worldly alliances. I much prefer the company of ploughboys and tin-peddlers, to the silken and perfumed amity which celebrates its days of encounter by a frivolous display, by rides in a curricle, and dinners at the best taverns.

"Friendship," *Essays*, First Series (1841, repr. 1847).

See also RELATIONSHIPS

I must feel pride in my friend's accomplishments as if they were mine,— and a property in his virtues. I feel as warmly when he is praised, as the lover when he hears applause of his engaged maiden.

"Friendship," *Essays*, First Series (1841, repr. 1847).

Let it be an alliance of two large, formidable natures, mutually beheld, mutually feared, before yet they recognize the deep identity which beneath these disparities unites them.

"Friendship," *Essays*, First Series (1841, repr. 1847).

Men have sometimes exchanged names with their friends, as if they would signify that in their friend each loved his own soul.

"Friendship," *Essays*, First Series (1841, repr. 1847).

Only be admonished by what you already see, not to strike leagues of friendship with cheap persons, where no friendship can be. Our impatience betrays us into rash and foolish alliances which no God attends.

"Friendship," *Essays*, First Series (1841, repr. 1847).

Our friendships hurry to short and poor conclusions, because we have made them a texture of wine and dreams, instead of the tough fibre of the human heart. The laws of friendship are austere and eternal, of one web with the laws of nature and of morals.

"Friendship," *Essays*, First Series (1841, repr. 1847).

The essence of friendship is entireness, a total magnanimity and trust. It must not surmise or provide for infirmity. It treats its object as a god, that it might deify both.

"Friendship," *Essays*, First Series (1841, repr. 1847).

Treat your friend as a spectacle.

"Friendship," *Essays*, First Series (1841, repr. 1847).

We over-estimate the conscience of our friend. His goodness seems better than our goodness, his nature finer, his temptations less. Everything that is his,—his name, his form, his dress, books, and instruments,—fancy enhances. Our own thought sounds new and larger from his mouth.

"Friendship," *Essays*, First Series (1841, repr. 1847).

Who hears me, who understands me, becomes mine,—a possession for all time.

"Friendship," *Essays*, First Series (1841, repr. 1847).

GENIUS

But genius looks forward: the eyes of man are set in his forehead, not in his hindhead: man hopes: genius creates. Whatever talents may be, if man create not, the pure efflux of the Deity is not his;—cinders and smoke there may be, but not yet flame.

"The American Scholar," repr. in *Emerson: Essays and Lectures*, ed. Joel Porte (1983).

Oration, August 31, 1837, delivered before the Phi Beta Kappa Society, Cambridge, Massachusetts.

See also CREATIVITY

Genius is its own end.

"The Method of Nature," *Nature, Addresses, and Lectures* (1849).

Speech, August 11, 1841, at Waterville College, Maine before the Society of the Adelphi.

But genius is religious. It is a larger imbibing of the common heart.

"The Over-Soul," *Essays*, First Series (1841, repr. 1847).

Great geniuses have the shortest biographies. Their cousins can tell you nothing about them. They lived in their writings, and so their house and street life was trivial and commonplace. If you would know their tastes and complexions, the most admiring of their readers most resembles them.

"Plato; or, the Philosopher," *Representative Men* (1850).

The young man reveres men of genius, because, to speak truly, they are more himself than he is.

"The Poet," *Essays*, Second Series (1844).

See also YOUTH

To believe your own thought, to believe that what is true for you in your private heart is true for all men,—that is genius.

"Self-Reliance," *Essays*, First Series (1841, repr. 1847).

But genius is the power to labor better and more availably. Deserve thy genius: exalt it.

"The Transcendentalist," repr. in *The Portable Emerson*, ed. Carl Bode (1946, repr. 1981).

Speech, January 1842, at the Masonic Temple in Boston, repr. in *The Dial* (1843) and *Nature, Addresses, and Lectures* (1849).

Universities are, of course, hostile to geniuses, which seeing and using ways of their own, discredit the routine: as churches and monasteries persecute youthful saints.

"Universities," *English Traits* (1856).

See also UNIVERSITIES AND COLLEGES

GIFTS

But it is a cold, lifeless business when you go to the shops to buy something, which does not represent your life and talent, but a gold-smith's.

"Gifts," *Essays*, Second Series (1844).

He is a good man, who can receive a gift well. We are either glad or sorry at a gift, and both emotions are unbecoming.

"Gifts," *Essays*, Second Series (1844).

If, at any time, it comes into my head, that a present is due from me to somebody, I am puzzled what to give, until the opportunity is gone.

"Gifts," *Essays*, Second Series (1844).

GOD

There is never a beginning, there is never an end, to the inexplicable continuity of this web of God, but always circular power returning into itself.

"The American Scholar," repr. In *Emerson: Essays and Lectures*, ed. Joel Porte (1983).

Oration, August 31, 1837, delivered before the Phi Beta Kappa Society, Cambridge, Massachusetts.

See also POWER

If the red slayer think he slays,
Or if the slain think he is slain,
They know not well the subtle ways
I keep, and pass, and turn again.

"Brahma," *May-Day and Other Pieces* (1867).

The first version of this was called "Song of the Soul."

Put God in your debt. Every stroke shall be repaid. The longer the payment is withholden, the better for you; for compound interest on compound interest is the rate and usage of this exchequer.

"Compensation," *Essays*, First Series (1841, repr. 1847).

See also DEBT

The true doctrine of omnipresence is, that God reappears with all his parts in every moss and cobweb.

"Compensation," *Essays*, First Series (1841, repr. 1847).

See also CREATION, THE

Dare to love God without mediator or veil.

"The Divinity School Address," repr. In *Emerson: Essays and Lectures*, ed. Joel Porte (1983).

Address, July 15, 1838, delivered before the senior class in Divinity College, Cambridge.

The time is coming when all men will see that the gift of God to the soul is not a vaunting, overpowering, excluding sanctity, but a sweet, natural goodness, a goodness like thine and mine, and that so invites thine and mine to be and to grow.

"The Divinity School Address," repr. in *The Portable Emerson*, ed. Carl Bode (1946, repr. 1981).

Address, July 15, 1838, delivered before the senior class in Divinity College, Cambridge.

See also HUMAN DEVELOPMENT

These facts have always suggested to man the sublime creed that the world is not the product of manifold power, but of one will, of one mind; and that one mind is everywhere active, in each ray of the star, in each wavelet of the pool; and whatever opposes that will is everywhere balked and baffled, because things are made so, and not otherwise.

"The Divinity School Address," repr. in *The Portable Emerson*, ed. Carl Bode (1946, repr. 1981).

Address, July 15, 1838, delivered before the senior class in Divinity College, Cambridge.

Life is a series of surprises, and would not be worth taking or keeping, if it were not. God delights to isolate us every day, and hide from us the past and the future.

"Experience," *Essays*, Second Series (1844).

We see God face to face every hour, and know the savor of Nature.

"Illusions," *The Conduct of Life* (1860).

See also NATURE

Standing on the bare ground,—my head bathed by the blithe air, and uplifted into infinite space,—all mean egotism vanishes. I become a transparent eye-ball; I am nothing; I see all; the currents of the Universal Being circulate through me; I am part and particle of God.

Nature, ch. 1, (1836, revised and repr. 1849).

This is perhaps Emerson's most famous passage and an index to his notion of the individual's connection to the Divine as well as to his ultimate vision of true knowing. The image of the transparent eyeball is perhaps difficult to summarize, but it clearly ought to dissuade any simplistic ideas of Emersonian individualism.

See also CREATION, THE

Man is a stream whose source is hidden. Our being is descending into us from we know not whence. The most exact calculator has no prescience that somewhat incalculable may not balk the very next moment. I am constrained every moment to acknowledge a higher origin for events than the will I call mine.

"The Over-Soul," *Essays*, First Series (1841, repr. 1847).

We live in succession, in division, in parts, in particles. Meantime within man is the soul of the whole; the wise silence; the universal beauty, to which every particle is equally related; the eternal ONE.

"The Over-Soul," *Essays*, First Series (1841, repr. 1847).

See also ETERNITY

When we have broken our god of tradition, and ceased from our god of rhetoric, then may God fire the heart with his presence.

"The Over-Soul," *Essays*, First Series (1841, repr. 1847).

See also RELIGION

Give me the eye to see a navy in an acorn. What is there of the divine in a load of bricks? What of the divine in a barber's shop or a privy? Much, all.

Quoted in Robert D. Richardson, Jr., *Emerson: The Mind on Fire*, ch. 29, (1995).

Let us stun and astonish the intruding rabble of men and books and institutions by a simple declaration of the divine fact. Bid the invaders take the shoes from off their feet, for God is here within.

"Self-Reliance," *Essays*, First Series (1841, repr. 1847).

When a man lives with God, his voice shall be as sweet as the murmur of the brook and the rustle of the corn.

"Self-Reliance," *Essays*, First Series (1841, repr. 1847).

Belief and love,—a believing love will relieve us of a vast load of care. O my brothers, God exists. There is a soul at the centre of nature, and over the will of every man, so that none of us can wrong the universe.

"Spiritual Laws," *Essays*, First Series (1841, repr. 1847).

See also CREATION, THE

GOVERNMENT

Government exists to defend the weak and the poor and the injured party; the rich and the strong can better take care of themselves.

"Address Delivered in Concord on the Anniversary of the Emancipation of the Negroes in the British West Indies, August 1, 1844," *Miscellanies* (1883, repr. 1904).

To educate the wise man, the State exists; and with the appearance of the wise man, the State expires. The appearance of character makes the state unnecessary. The wise man is the State.

"Politics," *Essays*, Second Series (1844).

See also WISDOM

What satire on government can equal the severity of censure conveyed in the word *politic*, which now for the ages has signified *cunning*, intimating that the state is a trick?

"Politics," *Essays*, Second Series (1844).

See also POLITICS

The wise and just man will always feel that he stands on his own feet; that he imparts strength to the state, not receives security from it; and if all went down, he and such as he would quite easily combine in a new and better constitution.

"The Young American," *Nature, Addresses, and Lectures* (1849).

The message here anticipates the spirit of JFK's "Ask not what your country can do for you, but what you can do for your country." Speech, February 7, 1844, the Mercantile Library Association, Boston, Massachusetts.

See also SOCIETY

GREATNESS

A great man scarcely knows how he dines, how he dresses; but without railing or precision, his living is natural and poetic.

"Heroism," *Essays*, First Series (1841, repr. 1847).

Great men or men of great gifts you shall easily find, but symmetrical men never.

"Nominalist and Realist," *Essays*, Second Series (1844).

To be great is to be misunderstood.

"Self-Reliance," *Essays*, First Series (1841, repr. 1847).

HAPPINESS

Health, south wind, books, old trees, a boat, a friend.

Emerson in His Journals, March 1847, ed. Joel Porte (1982).

To fill the hour,—that is happiness; to fill the hour, and leave no crevice for a repentance or an approval. We live amid surfaces, and the true art of life is to skate well on them.

"Experience," *Essays*, Second Series (1844).

Heroes and Heroines

The hero sees that the event is ancillary: it must follow *him*.

"Character," *Essays*, Second Series (1844).

But whoso is heroic will always find crises to try his edge.

"Heroism," *Essays*, First Series (1841, repr. 1847).

Heroism works in contradiction to the voice of mankind, and in contradiction, for a time, to the voice of the great and the good.

"Heroism," *Essays*, First Series (1841, repr. 1847).

Emerson also says ". . . every heroic act measures itself by its contempt of some external good." See Kierkegaard's essay "Fear and Trembling" for an elaboration of this idea that the hero may be called to undermine common standards of morality.

The hero is a mind of such balance that no disturbances can shake his will, but pleasantly, and, as it were, merrily, he advances to his own music, alike in frightful alarms and in the tipsy mirth of universal dissoluteness.

"Heroism," *Essays*, First Series (1841, repr. 1847).

History

The history of mankind interests us only as it exhibits a steady gain of truth and right, in the incessant conflict which it records between the material and the moral nature.

"Address Delivered in Concord on the Anniversary of the Emancipation of the Negroes in the British West Indies, August 1, 1844," *Miscellanies* (1883, repr. 1904).

All history becomes subjective; in other words there is properly no history, only biography.

"History," *Essays*, First Series (1841, repr. 1847).

I have no expectation that any man will read history aright who thinks that what has been done in a remote age, by men whose names have resounded far, has any deeper sense than what he is doing to-day.

"History," *Essays*, First Series (1841, repr. 1847).

$\mathcal{H}$OPE

Hitch your wagon to a star.

"Civilization," *Society and Solitude* (1870).

We judge of a man's wisdom by his hope, knowing that the inexhaustibleness of nature is an immortal youth.

"Spiritual Laws," *Essays*, First Series (1841, repr. 1847).

See also WISDOM

$\mathcal{H}$UMAN DEVELOPMENT

A man is a method, a progressive arrangement; a selecting principle, gathering his like to him; wherever he goes.

"Spiritual Laws," *Essays*, First Series (1841, repr. 1847).

See also MANKIND

$\mathcal{H}$UMILITY

A man in the view of absolute goodness, adores, with total humility. Every step downward, is a step upward. The man who renounces himself, comes to himself.

"The Divinity School Address," repr. in *The Portable Emerson*, ed. Carl Bode (1946, repr. 1981). Address, July 15, 1838, delivered before the senior class in Divinity College, Cambridge.

This quotation recommends a more subtle understanding of Emersonian individualism. Emerson does not envisage solitary, selfish, anti-communitarians. Rather his brand of individualism is founded upon humility and a self-renunciation that eventually finds itself again in a profound connection to all of creation.

See also SELF

*I*DEALISM

In the actual world—the painful kingdom of time and place—dwell care, and canker, and fear. With thought, with the ideal, is immortal hilarity, the rose of joy.

"Love," *Essays*, First Series (1841, repr. 1847).

Every materialist will be an idealist; but an idealist can never go backward to be a materialist.

"The Transcendentalist," repr. in *The Portable Emerson*, ed. Carl Bode (1946, repr. 1981).

Speech, January 1842, at the Masonic Temple in Boston, repr. in *The Dial* (1843) and *Nature, Addresses, and Lectures* (1849).

*I*LLUSIONS

Life will show you masks that are worth all of your carnivals.

"Illusions," *The Conduct of Life* (1860).

*I*MAGINATION

If I could put my hand on the north star, would it be as beautiful? The sea is lovely, but when we bathe in it the beauty forsakes all the near water. For the imagination and senses cannot be gratified at the same time.

"Beauty," *The Conduct of Life* (1860).

There are no days in life so memorable as those which vibrated to some stroke of the imagination.

"Beauty," *The Conduct of Life* (1860).

We live by our imaginations, by our admirations, by our sentiments. The child walks amid heaps of illusions, which he does not like to have disturbed. The boy, how sweet to him his fancy! how dear the story of barons and battles! What a hero he is, whilst he feeds on his heroes! What a debt is his to imaginative books!

"Illusions," *The Conduct of Life* (1860).
See also BOOKS

But the quality of the imagination is to flow, and not to freeze.

"The Poet," *Essays,* Second Series (1844).

This insight, which expresses itself by what is called Imagination, is a very high sort of seeing, which does not come by study, but by the intellect being where and what it sees, by sharing the path, or circuit of things through forms, and so making them translucid to others.

"The Poet," *Essays,* Second Series (1844).

INDEPENDENCE

He only is rich who owns the day.

"Works and Days," *Society and Solitude* (1870).

INDIVIDUALISM

It is not what talents or genius a man has, but how he is to his talents, that constitutes friendship and character. The man that stands by himself, the universe stands by him also.

"Behavior," *The Conduct of Life* (1860).
See also CHARACTER

An individual is an encloser. Time and space, liberty and necessity, truth and thought, are left at large no longer.

"Character," *Essays,* Second Series (1844).

We fancy men are individuals; so are pumpkins; but every pumpkin in the field, goes through every point of pumpkin history.

"Nominalist and Realist," *Essays,* Second Series (1844).
See also HUMANITY

We early arrive at the great discovery that there is one mind common to all individual men: that what is individual is less than what is universal ... that error, vice and disease have their seat in the superficial or individual nature.

Quoted in Robert D. Richardson Jr., *Emerson: The Mind on Fire*, ch. 42, (1995).

This is an essential articulation of Emersonian individualism. It comes from the first of a series of 12 lectures delivered in Boston beginning in December 1836.

For nonconformity the world whips you with its displeasure.

"Self-Reliance," *Essays*, First Series (1841, repr. 1847).

Is not a man better than a town?

"Self-Reliance," *Essays*, First Series (1841, repr. 1847).

Let him be great, and love shall follow him. Nothing is more deeply punished than the neglect of the affinities by which alone society should be formed, and the insane levity of choosing associates by others' eyes.

"Spiritual Laws," *Essays*, First Series (1841, repr. 1847).

See also GREATNESS

Now every one must do after his kind, be he asp or angel, and these must.

"The Transcendentalist," repr. in *The Portable Emerson*, ed. Carl Bode (1946, repr. 1981).

Speech, January 1842, at the Masonic Temple in Boston, repr. in *The Dial* (1843) and *Nature, Addresses, and Lectures* (1849).

The height, the deity of man is to be self-sustained, to need no gift, no foreign force. Society is good when it does not violate me, but best when it is likest to solitude.

"The Transcendentalist," repr. in *The Portable Emerson*, ed. Carl Bode (1946, repr. 1981).

Speech, January 1842, at the Masonic Temple in Boston, repr. in *The Dial* (1843) and *Nature, Addresses, and Lectures* (1849).

See also SOLITUDE

*I*NFANTS

Infancy is the perpetual Messiah, which comes into the arms of fallen men, and pleads with them to return to paradise.

Nature, ch. 8, (1836, revised and repr. 1849).

Infancy conforms to nobody: all conform to it, so that one babe commonly makes four or five out of the adults who prattle and play to it.

"Self-Reliance," *Essays*, First Series (1841, repr. 1847).

In *Big Sur,* Jack Kerouac quotes the first part of this statement, turning it into an American Zen koan. Kerouac called Emerson the "trumpet of the morning in America."

INFINITY

For it is only the finite that has wrought and suffered; the infinite lies stretched in smiling repose.

"Spiritual Laws," *Essays*, First Series (1841, repr. 1847).

See also SUFFERING

INFLUENCES

A man is the whole encyclopedia of facts.

"History," *Essays*, First Series (1841, repr. 1847).

See also FACTS

There is one mind common to all individual men. Every man is an inlet to the same and to all of the same.

"History," *Essays*, First Series (1841, repr. 1847).

See also SELF

Exhaust them, wrestle with them, let them not go until their blessing be won, and, after a short season, the dismay will be overpast, the excess of influence withdrawn, and they will be no longer an alarming meteor, but one more brighter star shining serenely in your heaven, and blending its light with all your day.

"Intellect," *Essays*, First Series (1841, repr. 1847).

Here Emerson anticipates Harold Bloom's theory of literary creation as a wrestling with one's literary fathers and mothers.

See also WRITERS AND WRITING

INSTITUTIONS

No institution will be better than the institutor.

"Character," *Essays*, Second Series (1844).

Being a philosopher concerned with the broader implications of education, Emerson was probably making a pun on "tutor" and "institutor."

The wave of evil washes all our institutions alike.

"New England Reformers," *Essays*, Second Series (1844).

Lecture, March 3, 1844, in Amory Hall, Boston, Massachusetts.

INTEGRITY

A little integrity is better than any career.

"Behavior," *The Conduct of Life* (1860).

See also CHARACTER

A man should give us a sense of mass.

"Character," *Essays*, Second Series (1844).

INTELLECTUALS

In this distribution of functions, the scholar is the delegated intellect. In the right state, he is, *Man Thinking*. In the degenerate state, when the victim of society, he tends to become a mere thinker, or, still worse, the parrot of other men's thinking.

"The American Scholar," repr. In *Emerson: Essays and Lectures*, ed. Joel Porte (1983).

Here Emerson anticipates Wittgenstein's advice to his young philosophy students not to become professional philosophers, but to leave the academy and take up a vocation.

See also WORK

Inaction is cowardice, but there can be no scholar without the heroic mind.

"The American Scholar," repr. In *Emerson: Essays and Lectures*, ed. Joel Porte (1983).

Beware when the great God lets loose a thinker on this planet. Then all things are at risk.

"Circles," *Essays*, First Series (1847).

A Scholar is a candle which the love & desire of men will light. Let it not lie in a dark box.

Emerson in His Journals, March 25, 1847, ed. Joel Porte (1982).

See also GOD

Intellectual tasting of life will not supersede muscular activity. If a man should consider the nicety of the passage of a piece of bread down his throat, he would starve.

"Experience," *Essays*, Second Series (1844).

See also ACTION

People disparage knowing and the intellectual life, and urge doing. I am content with knowing, if only I could know.

"Experience," *Essays*, Second Series (1844).

See also KNOWLEDGE

We hear eagerly every thought and word quoted from an intellectual man. But in his presence our own mind is roused to activity, and we forget very fast what he says.

"Fate," *The Conduct of Life* (1860).

A self-denial, no less austere than the saint's, is demanded of the scholar. He must worship truth, and forgo all things for that, and choose defeat and pain, so that his treasure in thought is thereby augmented.

"Intellect," *Essays*, First Series (1841, repr. 1847).

What is addressed to us for contemplation does not threaten us, but makes us intellectual beings.

"Intellect," *Essays*, First Series (1841, repr. 1847).

See also THINKING AND THOUGHT

The scholar may lose himself in schools, in words, and become a pedant; but when he comprehends his duties, he above all men is a realist, and converses with things.

"Literary Ethics," *Nature, Addresses, and Lectures* (1849).

Speech, July 24, 1838, at Dartmouth College.

In literary circles, the men of trust and consideration, bookmakers, editors, university deans and professors, bishops, too, were by no means men of the largest literary talent, but usually of a low and ordinary intellectuality, with a sort of mercantile activity and working talent. Indifferent hacks and mediocrities tower, by pushing their forces to a lucrative point, or by working power, over multitudes of superior men, in Old as in New England.

"Power," *The Conduct of Life* (1860).

The intellectual life may be kept clean and healthful, if man will live the life of nature, and not import into his mind difficulties which are none of his.

"Spiritual Laws," *Essays*, First Series (1841, repr. 1847).

*I*NTUITION

Every known fact in natural science was divined by the presentiment of somebody, before it was actually verified.

"Nature," *Essays*, Second Series (1844).

See also FACTS

He will perceive that there are far more excellent qualities in the student than preciseness and infallibility; that a guess is often more fruitful than an indisputable affirmation, and that a dream may let us deeper into the secret of nature than a hundred concerted experimenters.

Nature, ch. 8, (1836, revised and repr. 1849).

See also SCIENCE

We denote this primary wisdom as Intuition, whilst all later teachings are tuitions.

"Self-Reliance," *Essays*, First Series (1841, repr. 1847).

One of Emerson's more celebrated puns. Here, Emerson speaks especially to educators, as he attempts to erode the dominance of the rational wherever we seek to teach and to learn. In "The Poet," he will say essentially the same thing when he chides the artist to throw up his reigns and trust to the instinct of his horse.

JESUS CHRIST

Jesus Christ belonged to the true race of the prophets. He saw with an open eye the mystery of the soul. Drawn by its severe harmony, ravished with its beauty, he lived in it, and had his being there. Alone in all history he estimated the greatness of man.

"The Divinity School Address," repr. in *The Portable Emerson*, ed. Carl Bode (1946, repr. 1981).

Address, July 15, 1838, delivered before the senior class in Divinity College, Cambridge.

For I choose that my remembrances of him should be pleasing, affecting, religious. I will love him as a glorified friend, after the free way of friendship, and not pay him a stiff sign of respect, as men do to those whom they fear. A passage read from his discourses, a moving provocation to works like his, any act or meeting which tends to awaken a pure thought, a flow of love, an original design of virtue, I call a worthy, a true commemoration.

"The Lord's Supper," *Miscellanies*, (1883, repr. 1904).

Sermon preached on Sept. 9, 1832 at Second Church, Boston, Massachussetts.

He is the mediator in that only sense in which possibly any being can mediate between God and man,—that is, an instructor of man. He teaches us how to become like God.

"The Lord's Supper," *Miscellanies*, (1883, repr. 1904).

Sermon given on September 9, 1832 at the Second Church, Boston, Massachusetts.

The visible heavens and earth sympathize with Jesus.

Nature, ch. 3, (1836, revised and repr. 1849).

See also NATURE

The dogma of the mystic offices of Christ being dropped, and he standing on his genius as a moral teacher, 'tis impossible to maintain the old emphasis of his personality; and it recedes, as all persons must, before the sublimity of the moral laws.

"Worship," *The Conduct of Life* (1860).

JOY

Come out of the azure. Love the day. Do not leave the sky out of your landscape.

"Behavior," *The Conduct of Life* (1860).

See also LIFE

KNOWLEDGE

And, in fine, the ancient precept, "Know thyself," and the modern precept, "Study nature," become at last one maxim.

"The American Scholar," repr. in *Emerson: Essays and Lectures*, ed. Joel Porte (1983).

Oration, August 31, 1837, delivered before the Phi Beta Kappa Society, Cambridge, Massachusetts.

See also SELF

I embrace the common, I explore and sit at the feet of the familiar, the low. Give me insight into to-day, and you may have the antique and future worlds.

"The American Scholar," repr. in *Emerson: Essays and Lectures*, ed. Joel Porte (1983).

Oration, August 31, 1837, delivered before the Phi Beta Kappa Society, Cambridge, Massachusetts.

It is a mischievous notion that we are come late into nature; that the world was finished a long time ago. As the world was plastic and fluid in the hands of God, so it is ever to so much of his attributes as we bring to it. To ignorance and sin, it is flint. They adapt themselves to it as they may; but in proportion as a man has anything in him divine, the firmament flows before him and takes his signet and form.

"The American Scholar," repr. in *Emerson: Essays and Lectures*, ed. Joel Porte (1983).

This summarizes Emerson's theory of knowledge, owing much to Kant's theory of mental categories, but also anticipating the 20th-century religious philosopher Owen Barfield, who argues that in acts of perception, we co-create the world with the Divine.

See also CREATION, THE

Life is our dictionary.

"The American Scholar," repr. in *Emerson: Essays and Lectures*, ed. Joel Porte (1983).

Oration, August 31, 1837, delivered before the Phi Beta Kappa Society, Cambridge, Massachusetts.

See also ACTION

The world is nothing, the man is all; in yourself is the law of all nature, and you know not yet how a globule of sap ascends; in yourself slumbers the whole of Reason; it is for you to know all, it is for you to dare all.

"The American Scholar," repr. in *Emerson: Essays and Lectures*, ed. Joel Porte (1983).

Oration, August 31, 1837, delivered before the Phi Beta Kappa Society, Cambridge, Massachusetts.

See also MANKIND

Thus to him, to this school-boy under the bending dome of day, is suggested, that he and it proceed from one root; one is leaf and one is flower; relation, sympathy, stirring in every vein. And what is that Root? Is not that the soul of his soul?—A thought too bold,—a dream too wild.

"The American Scholar," repr. in *Emerson: Essays and Lectures*, ed. Joel Porte (1983).

Oration, August 31, 1837, delivered before the Phi Beta Kappa Society, Cambridge, Massachusetts.

See also NATURE

All I know is reception; I am and I have: but I do not get, and when I fancied I had gotten anything, I found I did not.

"Experience," *Essays*, Second Series (1844).

There are as many pillows of illusion as flakes in a snow-storm. We wake from one dream into another dream.

"Illusions," *The Conduct of Life* (1860).

See also ILLUSIONS

All our progress is an unfolding, like the vegetable bud. You first have an instinct, then an opinion, then a knowledge, as the plant has root, bud, and fruit. Trust the instinct to the end, though you can render no reason. It is vain to hurry it. By trusting it to the end, it shall ripen into truth, and you shall know why you believe.

"Intellect," *Essays*, First Series (1841, repr. 1847).

I am present at the sowing of the seed of the world. With a geometry of sunbeams, the soul lays the foundations of nature.

"Intellect," *Essays*, First Series (1841, repr. 1847).

See also SOUL

Explore, and explore. Be neither chided nor flattered out of your position of perpetual inquiry. Neither dogmatize, or accept another's dogmatism.

"Literary Ethics," *Nature, Addresses, and Lectures* (1849).

Speech, July 24, 1838, at Dartmouth College.

By degrees we may come to know the primitive sense of the permanent objects of nature, so that the world shall be to us an open book, and every form significant of its hidden life and final cause.

Nature, ch. 4, (1836, revised and repr. 1849).

See also NATURE

Every moment instructs, and every object: for wisdom is infused into every form. It has been poured into us as blood; it convulsed us as pain; it slid into us as pleasure; it enveloped us in dull, melancholy days, or in days of cheerful labor; we did not guess its essence, until after a long time.

"Nature," *Essays*, Second Series (1844).

The shows of the day, the dewy morning, the rainbow, mountains, orchards in blossom, stars, moonlight, shadows in still water, and the like, if too eagerly hunted, become shows merely, and mock us with their unreality.

Nature, ch. 3, (1836, revised and repr. 1849).

Here Emerson articulates his vision of knowing as form of receptivity, rather than a grasping activity. Instead of saying "I've got it" when we understand something, Emerson would have us say "It has got me."

See also NATURE

We live in a system of approximations. Every end is prospective of some other end, which is also temporary; a round and final success nowhere. We are encamped in nature, not domesticated.

"Nature," *Essays*, Second Series (1844).

Emerson anticipates John Dewey's version of the pragmatic mode of knowing as a continuous, endless and ever-blossoming investigation.

The only mode of obtaining an answer to these questions of the senses is to forego all low curiosity, and, accepting the tide of being which floats us into the secret of nature, work and live, work and live, and all unawares the advancing soul has built and forged for itself a new condition, and the question and the answer are one.

"The Over-Soul," *Essays*, First Series (1841, repr. 1847).

A moody child and wildly wise
Pursued the game with joyful eyes,

Which chose, like meteors, their way,
And rived the dark with private ray.

"The Poet," *Essays*, Second Series (1844).

See also PHILOSOPHY AND PHILOSOPHERS

I shun father and mother and wife and brother when my genius calls me. I would write on the lintels of the door-post, *Whim.* I hope that it is somewhat better than whim at last, but we cannot spend the day in explanation.

"Self-Reliance," *Essays*, First Series (1841, repr. 1847).

Compare with *Matthew* 10:37, where Jesus says: "Whoever loves father or mother more than me is not worthy of me; and whoever loves son or daughter more than me is not worthy of me." There are also clear links to *Genesis* 22:1–18, where Abraham leaves all of society behind him to sacrifice his son, Isaac.

LAND, THE

If a man own land, the land owns him.

"Wealth," *The Conduct of Life* (1860).

LANGUAGE

But wise men pierce this rotten diction and fasten words again to visible things; so that picturesque language is at once a commanding certificate that he who employs it, is a man in alliance with truth and God.

Nature, ch. 4, (1836, revised and repr. 1849).

Quotations such as this can be used to counter the common assumption that Emerson was a feathery, abstract idealist. For Emerson, a person who truly speaks is rooted in the particulars of the world and thus speaks a concrete language. See his thoughts on nature and spirituality, for he clearly argues that the Divine, the human mind, and nature are bound together. To search for one, you must search for all.

The corruption of man is followed by the corruption of language.

Nature, ch. 4, (1836, revised and repr. 1849).

The world is emblematic. Parts of speech are metaphors, because the whole of nature is a metaphor of the human mind.

Nature, ch. 4, (1836, revised and repr. 1849).

See also NATURE

We are thus assisted by natural objects in the expression of particular meanings. But how great a language to convey such pepper-corn informations!

Nature, ch. 4, (1836, revised and repr. 1849).

Emerson muses that language may be more than a mere tool to signify objects. It might indeed transcend utility and embody in itself unheard-of regions of significance.

Words are finite organs of the infinite mind. They cannot cover the dimensions of what is in truth. They break, chop, and impoverish it.

Nature, ch. 5, (1836, revised and repr. 1849).

Clearly Emerson is ambivalent about the nature and uses of language.

The action of the soul is oftener in that which is felt and left unsaid, than in that which is said in any conversation. It broods over every society, and they unconsciously seek for it in each other.

"The Over-Soul," *Essays,* First Series (1841, repr. 1847).

Every word was once a poem. Every new relation is a new word.

"The Poet," *Essays,* Second Series (1844).

For all symbols are fluxional; all language is vehicular and transitive, and is good, as ferries and horses are, for conveyance, not as farms and houses are, for homestead.

"The Poet," *Essays,* Second Series (1844).

For, though the origin of most of our words is forgotten, each word was at first a stroke of genius, and obtained currency, because for the moment it symbolized the world to the first speaker and to the hearer. The etymologist finds the deadest word to have been once a brilliant picture.

"The Poet," *Essays,* Second Series (1844).

Words are also actions, and actions are a kind of words.

"The Poet," *Essays,* Second Series (1844).

See also ACTION

*L*EADERSHIP

Those who have ruled human destinies, like planets, for thousands of years, were not handsome men.

"Beauty," *The Conduct of Life* (1860).

The reason why men do not obey us, is because they see the mud at the bottom of our eye.

"Behavior," *The Conduct of Life* (1860).

Our chief want in life, is, someone who shall make us do what we can. This is the service of a friend. With him we are easily great.

"Considerations by the Way," *The Conduct of Life* (1860).

He who should inspire and lead his race must be defended from travelling with the souls of other men, from living, breathing, reading and writing in the daily, time-worn yoke of their opinions.

"Culture," *The Conduct of Life* (1860).

See also INDIVIDUALISM

But let us honestly state the facts. Our America has a bad name for superficialness. Great men, great nations, have not been boasters and buffoons, but perceivers of the terror of life, and have manned themselves to face it.

"Fate," *The Conduct of Life* (1860).

See also STRENGTH

A feeble man can see the farms that are fenced and tilled, the houses that are built. The strong man sees the possible houses and farms. His eye makes estates, as fast as the sun breeds clouds.

"Power," *The Conduct of Life* (1860).

See also STRENGTH

LIFE

I would study, I would know, I would admire forever.

"The Divinity School Address," repr. in *The Portable Emerson*, ed. Carl Bode (1946, repr. 1981).

Address, July 15, 1838, delivered before the senior class in Divinity College, Cambridge.

Life is not intellectual or critical, but sturdy. Its chief good is for well-mixed people who can enjoy what they find, without question.

"Experience," *Essays*, Second Series (1844).

See also INTELLECTUALS

The intellectual man requires a fine bait; the sots are easily amused. But everybody is drugged with his own frenzy, and the pageant marches at all hours, with music and banner and badge.

"Illusions," *The Conduct of Life* (1860).

See also INTELLECTUALS

The life of man is the true romance, which when it is valiantly conducted will yield the imagination a higher joy than any fiction.

"New England Reformers," *Essays*, Second Series (1844).

Lecture, March 3, 1844, in Amory Hall, Boston, Massachusetts.

Life wastes itself whilst we are preparing to live.

"Prudence," *Essays*, First Series (1841, repr. 1847).

'Tis a queer life, and the only humour proper to it seems quiet astonishment. Others laugh, weep, sell, or proselyte. I admire.

Quoted in Gay Wilson Allen, *Waldo Emerson*, (1981).

LITERATURE

How death-cold is literary genius before this fire of life!

"Character," *Essays*, Second Series (1844).

See also WRITERS AND WRITING

The use of literature is to afford us a platform whence we may command a view of our present life, a purchase by which we may move it.

"Circles," *Essays*, First Series (1841, repr. 1847).

There is no luck in literary reputation. They who make up the final verdict upon every book are not the partial and noisy readers of the hour when it appears; but a court as of angels, a public not to be bribed, not to be entreated, and not to be overawed, decides upon every man's title to fame. Only those books come down which deserve to last.

"Spiritual Laws," *Essays*, First Series (1841, repr. 1847).

See also BOOKS

*L*OVE

Love, and you shall be loved. All love is mathematically just, as much as the two sides of an algebraic equation.

"Compensation," *Essays*, First Series (1841, repr. 1847).

In the last analysis, love is only the reflection of a man's own worthiness from other men.

"Friendship," *Essays*, First Series (1841, repr. 1847).

See also FRIENDS AND FRIENDSHIP

It is thought a disgrace to love unrequited. But the great will see that true love cannot be unrequited. True love transcends the unworthy object, and dwells and broods on the eternal, and when the poor interposed mask crumbles, it is not sad, but feels rid of so much earth, and feels its independency the surer.

"Friendship," *Essays*, First Series (1841, repr. 1847).

See also IDEALISM

Love, which is the essence of God, is not for levity, but for the total worth of man.

"Friendship," *Essays*, First Series (1841, repr. 1847).

Give all to love:
Obey thy heart;
Friends, kindred, days,
Estate, good-fame,
Plans, credit, and the Muse,—
Nothing refuse.

"Give All to Love," *Poems* (1847).

Love prays. It makes covenants with Eternal Power in behalf of this dear mate.

"Love," *Essays*, First Series (1841, repr. 1847).

See also GOD

We must be lovers, and at once the impossible becomes possible.

"Man the Reformer," *Nature, Addresses, and Lectures* (1849).

Speech, January 25, 1841, before the Mechanics' Apprentices' Library Association, Boston, Massachusetts.

Lovers should guard their strangeness. If they forgive too much, all slides into confusion and meanness.

"Manners," *Essays,* Second Series (1844).

$\mathcal{M}$ANKIND

The life of man is a self-evolving circle, which, from a ring imperceptibly small, rushes on all sides outwards to new and larger circles, and that without end.

"Circles," *Essays,* First Series (1841, repr. 1847).

See also ETERNITY

A man is a golden impossibility. The line he must walk is a hair's breadth.

"Experience," *Essays,* Second Series (1844).

Man is the broken giant, and in all his weakness both his body and his mind are invigorated by habits of conversation with nature.

"History," *Essays,* First Series (1841, repr. 1847).

See also NATURE

There is nothing but is related to us, nothing that does not interest us,— kingdom, college, tree, horse, or iron show,—the roots of all things are in man.

"History," *Essays,* First Series (1841, repr. 1847).

A man is a god in ruins. When men are innocent, life shall be longer, and shall pass into the immortal, as gently as we awake from dreams.

Nature, ch. 8, (1836, revised and repr. 1849).

Emerson says that a "certain poet" sang this to him. Gay Wilson Allen and others have speculated that this poet could have been Bronson Alcott, Plotinus, or Emerson himself.

See also IMMORTALITY

Man is the dwarf of himself.

Nature, ch. 8, (1836, revised and repr. 1849).

Nor has science sufficient humanity, so long as the naturalist overlooks the wonderful congruity which subsists between man and the world; of which he is lord, not because he is the most subtile inhabitant, but because he is its head and heart, and finds something of himself in every great and small thing, in every mountain stratum, in every new law of color, fact of astronomy, or atmospheric influence which observation or analysis lay open.

Nature, ch. 8, (1836, revised and repr. 1849).

See also SCIENCE

For we are not pans and barrows, nor even porters of the fire and torch-bearers, but children of the fire, made of it, and only the same divinity transmuted, and at two or three removes, when we know least about it.

"The Poet," *Essays,* Second Series (1844).

See also HUMANITY

*M*IDDLE CLASS, THE

Our age is very cheap and intelligible. Unroof any house, and you shall find it. The well-being consists in having a sufficiency of coffee and toast, with a daily newspaper; a well glazed parlor, with marbles, mirrors and centre-table; and the excitement of a few parties and a few rides in a year.

"Address Delivered in Concord on the Anniversary of the Emancipation of the Negroes in the British West Indies, August 1, 1844," *Miscellanies* (1883, repr. 1904).

But all great men come out of the middle classes. 'Tis better for the head; 'tis better for the heart.

"Considerations by the Way," *The Conduct of Life* (1860).

*M*IND, THE

To the young mind, every thing is individual, stands by itself. By and by, it finds how to join two things, and see in them one nature; then three, then three thousand; and so, tyrannized over by its own unifying instinct, it goes on tying things together, diminishing anomalies, discovering roots running underground, whereby contrary and remote things cohere, and flower out from one stem.

"The American Scholar," repr. in *Emerson: Essays and Lectures*, ed. Joel Porte (1983).

Oration, August 31, 1837, delivered before the Phi Beta Kappa Society, Cambridge, Massachusetts.

See also THINKING AND THOUGHT

Every natural fact is a symbol of some spiritual fact. Every appearance in nature corresponds to some state of the mind, and that state of the mind can only be described by presenting that natural appearance as its picture.

Nature, ch. 4, (1836, revised and repr. 1849).

See also KNOWLEDGE

Every spirit builds itself a house; and beyond its house a world; and beyond its world, a heaven. Know then that the world exists for you.

Nature, ch. 8, (1836, revised and repr. 1849).

It is a secret which every intellectual man quickly learns, that, beyond the energy of his possessed and conscious intellect, he is capable of a new energy (as of an intellect doubled on itself), by abandonment to the nature of things; that, beside his privacy of power as an individual man, there is a great public power, on which he can draw, by unlocking, at all risks, his human doors, and suffering the ethereal tides to roll and circulate through him: then is he caught up into the life of the Universe, his speech is thunder, his thought is law, and his words are universally intelligible as the plants and animals.

"The Poet," *Essays,* Second Series (1844).

See also INTELLIGENCE

Nothing is at last sacred but the integrity of your own mind.

"Self-Reliance," *Essays,* First Series (1841, repr. 1847).

Ministry, the

Yourself a newborn bard of the Holy Ghost, cast behind you all conformity, and acquaint men at first hand with Deity.

"Divinity School Address," repr. In *Emerson: Essays and Lectures*, ed. Joel Porte (1983).

Address, July 15, 1838, delivered before the senior class in Divinity College, Cambridge.

See also CONFORMITY

Preaching is the expression of the moral sentiment in application to the duties of life.

"The Divinity School Address," repr. in *The Portable Emerson*, ed. Carl Bode (1946, repr. 1981).

Address, July 15, 1838, delivered before the senior class in Divinity College, Cambridge.

The true preacher can be known by this, that he deals out to the people his life,—life passed through the fire of thought.

"The Divinity School Address," repr. in *The Portable Emerson*, ed. Carl Bode (1946, repr. 1981).

Address, July 15, 1838, delivered before the senior class in Divinity College, Cambridge.

It is my desire, in the office of a Christian minister, to do nothing which I cannot do with my whole heart. Having said this, I have said all.

"The Lord's Supper," *Miscellanies* (1883, repr. 1904).

Sermon, September 9, 1832, at the Second Church, Boston, Massachusetts.

Miracles

But the word Miracle, as pronounced by Christian churches, gives a false impression; it is Monster. It is not one with the blowing clover and falling rain.

"The Divinity School Address," repr. in *The Portable Emerson*, ed. Carl Bode (1946, repr. 1981).

Address, July 15, 1838, delivered before the senior class in Divinity College, Cambridge.

See also CHRISTIANITY AND CHRISTIANS

The world is the perennial miracle which the soul worketh.

"The Over-Soul," *Essays*, First Series (1841, repr. 1847).

See also CREATION, THE

$\mathcal{M}$OODS

Our moods do not believe in each other.

"Circles," *Essays*, First Series (1841, repr. 1847).

Life is a train of moods like a string of beads, and, as we pass through them, they prove to be many-colored lenses which paint the world their own hue, and each shows only what lies in its focus.

"Experience," *Essays*, Second Series (1844).

See also PERCEPTION

$\mathcal{M}$OTHERS

Men are what their mothers made them.

"Fate," *The Conduct of Life* (1860).

$\mathcal{N}$ATURE

The first in time and the first in importance of the influences upon the mind is that of nature. Every day, the sun; and after sunset, night and her stars. Ever the winds blow; ever the grass grows.

"The American Scholar," repr. In *Emerson: Essays and Lectures*, ed. Joel Porte (1983).

Oration, August 31, 1837, delivered before the Phi Beta Kappa Society, Cambridge, Massachusetts.

See also MIND, THE

Thus to him, to this schoolboy under the bending dome of day, is suggested that he and it proceed from one root; one is leaf and one is flower; relation, sympathy, stirring in every vein. And what is that root? Is not that the soul of his soul?

"The American Scholar," repr. In *Emerson: Essays and Lectures*, ed. Joel Porte (1983).

Oration, August 31, 1837, delivered before the Phi Beta Kappa Society, Cambridge, Massachusetts.

But Nature is no sentimentalist,—does not cosset or pamper us. We must see the world is rough and surly, and will not mind drowning a man or a woman; but swallows your ship like a grain of dust.

"Fate," *The Conduct of Life* (1860).

True Bramin, in the morning meadows wet,
Expound the Vedas of the violet.

"Gardener," *May-Day and Other Pieces* (1867).

In the woods in a winter afternoon one will see as readily the origin of the stained glass window, with which Gothic cathedrals are adorned, in the colors of the western sky seen through the bare and crossing branches of the forest.

"History," *Essays*, First Series (1841, repr. 1847).

See also CATHEDRALS

Nature is an endless combination and repetition of a very few laws. She hums the old well-known air through innumerable variations.

"History," *Essays*, First Series (1841, repr. 1847).

Every rational creature has all nature for his dowry and estate. It is his, if he will. He may divest himself of it; he may creep into a corner, and abdicate his kingdom, as most men do, but he is entitled to the world by his constitution.

Nature, ch. 3, (1836, revised and repr. 1849).

See also HUMANITY

How does Nature deify us with a few and cheap elements! Give me health and a day, and I will make the pomp of emperors ridiculous. The dawn is my Assyria; the sun-set and moon-rise my Paphos, and unimaginable realms of faerie; broad noon shall be my England of the senses and the understanding; the night shall be my Germany of mystic philosophy and dreams.

Nature, ch. 3, (1836, revised and repr. 1849).

See also CREATION, THE

I have no hostility to nature, but a child's love to it. I expand and live in the warm day like corn and melons.

Nature, ch. 6, (1836, revised and repr. 1849).

In the woods, is perpetual youth.

Nature, ch. 1, (1836, revised and repr. 1849).

See also YOUTH

Nature always wears the colors of the spirit. To a man laboring under calamity, the heat of his own fire hath sadness in it.

Nature, ch. 1, (1836, revised and repr. 1849).

By this Emerson means that as our moods change so too do our perceptions of the hues and shapes of nature. We are connected to the landscape and as we turn so does it.

Nature is a setting that fits equally well a comic or a mourning piece. In good health, the air is a cordial of incredible virtue. Crossing a bare common, in snow puddles, at twilight, under a clouded sky, without having in my thoughts any occurrence of special good fortune, I have enjoyed a perfect exhilaration. I am glad to the brink of fear.

Nature, ch. 1, (1836, revised and repr. 1849).

The last word "fear" invokes Kant's notion of the sublime in his essay "Anthropology from a Pragmatic Viewpoint," in which he defines the sublime as "that greatness in size and degree which arouses reverence. It invites us to approach it . . . but it deters (for instance, the thunder above our head, or mountains towering and savage) by causing us to fear that in comparison with it we are like nothing in our own estimation" (translated by Walter Cerf). See Kant's *Critique of Judgment*, especially the second book, "Analytic of the Sublime."

See also CREATION, THE

Nature is the symbol of the spirit.

Nature, ch. 4, (1836, revised and repr. 1849).

See also SOUL

Nature is thoroughly mediate. It is made to serve. It receives the dominion of man as meekly as the ass on which the Saviour rode. It offers all its kingdoms to man as the raw material which he may mould into what is useful. Man is never weary of working it up.

Nature, ch. 5, (1836, revised and repr. 1849).

This quotation might on its surface surprise some readers who believe that Emerson is the kind of environmentalist who is bent on leaving nature alone so humanity can learn from it. Like many religious thinkers, Emerson places the human mind and soul at the center of the universe. The key term here is "dominion," invoking *Genesis* 1:26 and suggesting wise, humble, connected, and responsible uses of the earth. Emerson is also proposing an epistemological theory here, namely that the world is created with every act of perception and thus humanity co-creates the world with God.

See also MIND, THE

Nature never wears a mean appearance. Neither does the wisest man extort her secret, and lose his curiosity by finding out all her perfection. Nature never became a toy to a wise spirit.

Nature, ch. 1, (1836, revised and repr. 1849).

See also SCIENCE

The first steps in Agriculture, Astronomy, Zoölogy (those first steps which the farmer, the hunter, and the sailor take), teach that nature's dice are always loaded; that in her heaps and rubbish are concealed sure and useful results.

Nature, ch. 5, (1836, revised and repr. 1849).

See also SCIENCE

To speak truly, few adult persons can see nature. Most persons do not see the sun. At least they have a very superficial seeing. The sun illuminates only the eye of the man, but shines into the eye and the heart of the child.

Nature, ch. 1, (1836, revised and repr. 1849).

See also WISDOM

Things admit of being used as symbols, because nature is a symbol, in the whole, and in every part.

"The Poet," *Essays,* Second Series (1844).

No ray is dimmed, no atom worn,
My oldest force is good as new,
And the fresh rose on yonder thorn
Gives back the bending heavens in dew.

"Song of Nature," *May-Day and Other Pieces* (1867).

*P*ARENTS AND PARENTHOOD

Respect the child. Wait and see the new product of Nature. Nature loves analogies, but not repetitions. Respect the child. Be not too much his parent. Trespass not on his solitude.

"Education," *Lectures and Biographical Sketches* (1883, repr. 1904).

*P*EACE

The triumphs of peace have been in some proximity to war.

"Power," *The Conduct of Life* (1860).

Nothing can bring you peace but yourself. Nothing can bring you peace but the triumph of principles.

"Self-Reliance," *Essays*, First Series (1841, repr. 1847).

My hours are peaceful centuries.

"Woodnotes II," *Poems* (1847).

So says Emerson, in the guise of a pine-tree.

*P*ERCEPTION

Our life is not so much threatened as our perception. Ghostlike we glide through nature, and should not know our place again.

"Experience," *Essays*, Second Series (1844).

Since everything in nature answers to a moral power, if any phenomenon remains brute and dark, it is that the corresponding faculty in the observer is not yet active.

"The Poet," *Essays*, Second Series (1844).

In other words, in every act of perception we are co-creators of the universe. Hence, if we find the world brutish, we are confronting such brutishness in ourselves.

My life is superficial, takes no root in the deep world; I ask, When shall I die, and be relieved of the responsibility of seeing a Universe which I do not use? I wish to exchange this flash-of-lightning faith for continuous daylight, this fever-glow for a benign climate.

"The Transcendentalist," repr. in *The Portable Emerson*, ed. Carl Bode (1946, repr. 1981).

Speech, January 1842, at the Masonic Temple in Boston, repr. in *The Dial* (1843) and *Nature, Addresses, and Lectures* (1849).

*P*HILOSOPHY

The poor and the low have their way of expressing the last facts of philosophy as well as you. "Blessed be nothing," and "The worse things are, the better they are," are proverbs which express the transcendentalism of common life.

"Circles," *Essays*, First Series (1841, repr. 1847).

Men are not philosophers, but are rather very foolish children, who, by reason of their partiality, see everything in the most absurd manner, and are the victims at all times of the nearest object. There is even no philosopher who is a philosopher at all times. Our experience, our perception is conditioned by the need to acquire in parts and in succession, that is, with every truth a certain falsehood.

"The Conservative," *Nature, Addresses, and Lectures* (1849).

Speech, December 9, 1841, at the Masonic Temple, Boston, Massachusetts.

See also KNOWLEDGE

But what help from these fineries or pedantries? What help from thought? Life is not dialectics. We, I think, in these times, have had lessons enough of the futility of criticism.

"Experience," *Essays*, Second Series (1844).

See also INTELLECTUALS

Whenever a true theory appears, it will be its own evidence. Its test is, that it will explain all phenomena.

Nature, Introduction, (1836, revised and repr. 1849).

See also TRUTH

A philosopher must be more than a philosopher.

"Plato; or, the Philosopher," *Representative Men* (1850).

*P*LANTS

Plants are the young of the world, vessels of health and vigor; but they grope ever upwards towards consciousness; the trees are imperfect men, and seem to bemoan their imprisonment, rooted in the ground.

"Nature," *Essays,* Second Series (1844).

The greatest delight which the fields and woods minister, is the suggestion of an occult relation between man and the vegetable. I am not alone and unacknowledged. They nod to me, and I to them.

Nature, ch. 1, (1836, revised and repr. 1849).

See also NATURE

*P*LEASURES

As soon as beauty is sought, not from religion and love, but for pleasure, it degrades the seeker.

"Art," *Essays,* First Series (1841, repr. 1847).

See also BEAUTY

We sell the thrones of angels for a short and turbulent pleasure.

"Circles," *Essays,* First Series (1841, repr. 1847).

The pleasure of life is according to the man that lives it, and not according to the work or the place.

"Fate," *The Conduct of Life* (1860).

There is more difference in the quality of our pleasures than in the amount.

"Prudence," *Essays,* First Series (1841, repr. 1847).

*P*OETRY AND POETS

There is some awe mixed with joy of our surprise, when this poet, who lived in some past world, two or three hundred years ago, says that which lies close to my own soul, that which I also had well nigh thought and said.

"The American Scholar," repr. In *Emerson: Essays and Lectures*, ed. Joel Porte (1983).

Oration, August 31, 1837, delivered before the Phi Beta Kappa Society, Cambridge, Massachusetts.

Therefore we value the poet. All the argument and all the wisdom is not in the encyclopedia, or the treatise on metaphysics, or the Body of Divinity, but in the sonnet or the play.

"Circles," *Essays*, First Series (1841, repr. 1847).

And of poetry, the success is not attained when it lulls and satisfies, but when it astonishes and fires us with new endeavours after the unattainable.

"Love," *Essays*, First Series (1841, repr. 1847).

The sensual man conforms thoughts to things; the poet conforms things to his thoughts. The one esteems nature as rooted and fast; the other, as fluid, and impresses his being thereon.

Nature, ch. 6, (1836, revised and repr. 1849).

The true philosopher and the true poet are one, and a beauty, which is truth, and a truth, which is beauty, is the aim of both.

Nature, ch. 6, (1836, revised and repr. 1849).

Ever since Plato banned poetry from the Republic, statements like this have been controversial, at least in the minds of philosophers. Here, Emerson anticipates the late 20th-century work in philosophy of literature, hermeneutics, and literary theory that seeks to heal the ancient rift between philosophy and poetry.

See also PHILOSOPHY AND PHILOSOPHERS

The great poet makes us feel our own wealth, and then we think less of his compositions. His best communication to our mind is to teach us to despise all he has done.

"The Over-Soul," *Essays*, First Series (1841, repr. 1847).

There is, in all great poets, a wisdom of humanity which is superior to any talents they exercise.

"The Over-Soul," *Essays*, First Series (1841, repr. 1847).

For it is not metres, but a metre-making argument, that makes a poem,—
a thought so passionate and alive, that, like the spirit of a plant or an
animal, it has an architecture of its own, and adorns nature with a new
thing.

"The Poet," *Essays*, Second Series (1844).

Emerson, anticipating post-modern philosophy, often grappled with what it meant to make an
argument. He questioned what narrow logical and philosophical modes of analysis actually
could achieve and surmised that art and whimsy and other "illogical" flights of the imagination
could also attempt to lend an accurate, or even true, picture of the way reality works and we
work in/on reality.

For, the experience of each new age requires a new confession, and the
world seems always waiting for its poet.

"The Poet," *Essays*, Second Series (1844).

See also ART AND ARTISTS

Language is fossil poetry.

"The Poet," *Essays*, Second Series (1844).

See also LANGUAGE

The breadth of the problem is great, for the poet is representative. He
stands among partial men for the complete man, and apprises us not of
his wealth, but of the commonwealth.

"The Poet," *Essays*, Second Series (1844).

See also ART AND ARTISTS

The poet alone knows astronomy, chemistry, vegetation, and animation,
for he does not stop at these facts, but employs them as signs. He knows
why the plain, or meadow of space, was strewn with these flowers we call
suns, and moons, and stars; why the great deep is adorned with animals,
with men, and gods; for, in every word he speaks he rides on them as the
horses of thought.

"The Poet," *Essays*, Second Series (1844).

See also SCIENCE

The poet is the person in whom these powers are in balance, the man
without impediment, who sees and handles that which others dream of,
traverses the whole scale of experience, and is representative of man, in
virtue of being the largest power to receive and to impart.

"The Poet," *Essays*, Second Series (1844).

The use of symbols has a certain power of emancipation and exhilaration for all men. We seem to be touched by a wand, which makes us dance and run about happily, like children. We are like persons who come out of a cave or cellar into the open air. This is the effect on us of tropes, fables, oracles, and all poetic forms. Poets are thus liberating gods.

"The Poet," *Essays,* Second Series (1844).

For, whom the Muses smile upon,
And touch with soft persuasion,
His words like a storm-wind can bring
Terror and beauty on their wing;
In his every syllable
Lurketh nature veritable.

"Saadi," *Poems* (1847).

Men consort in camp and town
But the poet dwells alone.

"Saadi," *Poems* (1847).
See also SOLITUDE

To the birds and trees he talks:
Caesar of his leafy Rome,
There the poet is at home.

"Woodnotes I," *Poems* (1847).
See also NATURE

What he knows nobody wants.
What he knows he hides, not vaunts.

"Woodnotes I," *Poems* (1847).

*P*OLITICS

The people know that they need in their representative much more than talent, namely, the power to make his talent trusted.

"Character," *Essays,* Second Series (1844).

A party is perpetually corrupted by personality.

"Politics," *Essays*, Second Series (1844).

Senators and presidents have climbed so high with pain enough, not because they think the place specially agreeable, but as an apology for real worth, and to vindicate their manhood in our eyes. This conspicuous chair is their compensation to themselves for being of a poor, cold, hard nature.

"Politics," *Essays*, Second Series (1844).

See also AMBITION

*P*OWER

Before we acquire great power we must acquire wisdom to use it well.

"Demonology," *Lectures and Biographical Sketches* (1883, repr. 1904).

See also WISDOM

Never mind the ridicule, never mind the defeat: up again, old heart!—it seems to say,—there is victory yet for all justice; and the true romance which the world exists to realize, will be the transformation of genius into practical power.

"Experience," *Essays*, Second Series (1844).

See also GENIUS

Power first, or no leading class. In politics and trade, bruisers and pirates are of better promise than talkers and clerks.

"Manners," *Essays*, Second Series (1844).

Power ceases in the instant of repose; it resides in the moment of transition from a past to a new state, in the shooting of the gulf, in the darting to an aim.

"Self-Reliance," *Essays*, First Series (1841, repr. 1847).

You think me the child of circumstance; I make my circumstance.

"The Transcendentalist," repr. in *The Portable Emerson*, ed. Carl Bode (1946, repr. 1981).

Speech, January 1842, at the Masonic Temple in Boston, repr. in *The Dial* (1843) and *Nature, Addresses, and Lectures* (1849).

See also SELF

PRAISE

I hate to be defended in a newspaper. As long as all that is said is said against me, I feel a certain assurance of success. But as soon as honeyed words of praise are spoken for me, I feel as one that lies unprotected before his enemies.

"Compensation," *Essays*, First Series (1841, repr. 1847).

You would compliment a coxcomb doing a good act, but you would not praise an angel. The silence that accepts merit as the most natural thing in the world, is the highest applause.

"The Divinity School Address," repr. in *The Portable Emerson*, ed. Carl Bode (1946, repr. 1981).

Address, July 15, 1838, delivered before the senior class in Divinity College, Cambridge.

PRAYER

Our prayers are prophets.

"Considerations by the Way," *The Conduct of Life* (1860).

In the moment when you make the least petition to God, though it be but a silent wish that he may approve you, or add one moment to your life,— do you not, in the very act, necessarily exclude all other beings from your thought? In that act, the soul stands alone with God, and Jesus is no more present to your mind than your brother or your child.

"The Lord's Supper," *Miscellanies* (1883, repr. 1904).

Sermon, September 9, 1832, at the Second Church, Boston, Massachusetts.

See also JESUS CHRIST

Is not prayer also a study of truth,—a sally of the soul into the unfound infinite? No man ever prayed heartily, without learning something. But when a faithful thinker, resolute to detach every object from personal relations, and see it in the light of thought, shall, at the same time, kindle science with the fire of the holiest affections, then will God go forth anew into creation.

Nature, ch. 8, (1836, revised and repr. 1849).

Emerson links science with religion in one, undivided mode of knowing.

See also SCIENCE

As soon as the man is at one with God, he will not beg. He will then see prayer in all action.

"Self-Reliance," *Essays,* First Series (1841, repr. 1847).

Prayer that craves a particular commodity, anything less than all good, is vicious.

"Self-Reliance," *Essays,* First Series (1841, repr. 1847).

$\mathcal{P}$RESENT, THE

Our life seems not present, so much as prospective; not for the affairs on which it is wasted, but as a hint of this vast-flowing vigor.

"Experience," *Essays,* Second Series (1844).

"Prospect" is a favorite word of Emerson's, implying, as it does, future fortunes, a place from which to gain an outlook, and a mining camp. All of these ideas can serve as metaphors for the Emersonian task.

But blest is he, who, playing deep, yet haply asks not why,
Too busied with the crowded hour to fear to live or die.

"Nature," *May-Day and Other Pieces* (1867).

But man postpones or remembers; he does not live in the present, but with reverted eye laments to the past, or, heedless of the riches that surround him, stands on tiptoe to foresee the future. He cannot be happy and strong until he too lives with nature in the present, above time.

"Self-Reliance," *Essays,* First Series (1841, repr. 1847).

It seems to be a rule of wisdom never to rely on your memory alone, scarcely even in acts of pure memory, but to bring the past for judgment into the thousand-eyed present, and live ever in a new day.

"Self-Reliance," *Essays,* First Series (1841, repr. 1847).

Write it on your heart that every day is the best day in the year. No man has learned anything rightly until he knows that every day is Doomsday.

"Works and Days," *Society and Solitude* (1870).

$\mathcal{P}$RIDE

The street is full of humiliations to the proud.

"Experience," *Essays*, Second Series (1844).

Man is timid and apologetic; he is no longer upright; he dares not say "I think," "I am," but quotes some saint or sage.

"Self-Reliance," *Essays*, First Series (1841, repr. 1847).

Emerson is clearly referring to Descartes' *cogito* argument, giving it a more heroic treatment than a traditional philosopher would.

Pride ruined the angels,
Their shame them restores;
And the joy that is sweetest
Lurks in stings of remorse.

"The Sphinx," *Poems* (1847).

$\mathcal{P}$ROPERTY

The charming landscape which I saw this morning is indubitably made up of some twenty or thirty farms. Miller owns this field, Locke that, and Manning the woodland beyond. But none of them owns the landscape. There is property in the horizon which no man has but he whose eye can integrate all parts, that is, the poet. This is the best part of these men's farms, yet to this their warranty-deeds give no title.

Nature, ch. 1, (1836, revised and repr. 1849).

While in college, Emerson struggled with and eventually rejected the writings of the British philosopher John Locke. We might take this passage to be a wry commentary on Locke's empiricism and his labor theory of value.

See also POETRY AND POETS

Things have their laws, as well as men; and things refuse to be trifled with. Property will be protected.

"Politics," *Essays*, Second Series (1844).

Whilst the rights of all as persons are equal, in virtue of their access to reason, their rights in property are very unequal. One man owns his clothes, and another owns a country.

"Politics," *Essays,* Second Series (1844).

See also WEALTH AND THE WEALTHY

QUOTATIONS

I quote another man's saying; unluckily, that other withdraws himself in the same way, and quotes me.

"Experience," *Essays,* Second Series (1844).

Every book is a quotation; and every house is a quotation out of all forests, and mines, and stone quarries; and every man is a quotation from all his ancestors.

"Plato; or, the Philosopher," *Representative Men* (1850).

Next to the originator of a good sentence is the first quoter of it. Many will read the book before one thinks of quoting a passage. As soon as he has done this, that line will be quoted east and west.

"Quotation and Originality," *Letters and Social Aims* (1875, repr. 1904).

We are as much informed of a writer's genius by what he selects as by what he originates. We read the quotation with his eyes, and find a new and fervent sense; as a passage from one of the poets, well recited, borrows new interest from the rendering. As the journals say, "the italics are ours."

"Quotation and Originality," *Letters and Social Aims* (1875, repr. 1904).

RACE

The civility of no race can be perfect whilst another race is degraded.

"Address Delivered in Concord on the Anniversary of the Emancipation of the Negroes in the British West Indies, August 1, 1844," *Miscellanies* (1883, repr. 1904).

The intellect,—that is miraculous! Who has it, has the talisman: his skin and bones, though they were of the color of night, are transparent, and the everlasting stars shine through, with attractive beams.

"Address Delivered in Concord on the Anniversary of the Emancipation of the Negroes in the British West Indies, August 1, 1844," *Miscellanies* (1883, repr. 1904).

See also MIND, THE

*R*EADING

One must be an inventor to read well.

"The American Scholar," repr. in *Emerson: Essays and Lectures*, ed. Joel Porte (1983).

Oration, August 31, 1837, delivered before the Phi Beta Kappa Society, Cambridge, Massachusetts.

See also BOOKS

The three practical rules, then, which I have to offer, are,— 1. Never read any book that is not a year old. 2. Never read any but famed books. 3. Never read any but what you like.

"Books," *Society and Solitude* (1870).

All that Shakespeare says of the king, yonder slip of a boy that reads in the corner feels to be true of himself.

"History," *Essays*, First Series (1841, repr. 1847).

Bookworm, break this sloth urbane;
A greater spirit bids thee forth
Than the gray dreams which thee detain.

"Monadnoc," *Poems* (1847).

See also BOOKS

How dare I read Washington's campaigns, when I have not answered the letters of my own correspondents? Is not that a just objection to much of our reading? It is a pusillanimous desertion of our work to gaze after our neighbours. It is peeping.

"Spiritual Laws," *Essays*, First Series (1841, repr. 1847).

I may say it of our preposterous use of books,—He knew not what to do, and so *he read.*

"Spiritual Laws," *Essays,* First Series (1841, repr. 1847).

See also BOOKS

You have observed a skilful man reading Virgil. Well, that author is a thousand books to a thousand persons. Take the book into your two hands, and read your eyes out; you will never find what I find.

"Spiritual Laws," *Essays,* First Series (1841, repr. 1847).

See also BOOKS

REASON

The great gifts are not got by analysis.

"Experience," *Essays,* Second Series (1844).

Logic is the procession or proportionate unfolding of the intuition; but its virtue is as silent method; the moment it would appear as propositions, and have a separate value, it is worthless.

"Intellect," *Essays,* First Series (1841, repr. 1847).

In his early journal entries, Emerson often admits he is not a logical machine that can churn out syllogistic pearls of wisdom. One might read his paeans to intuition as an attempt to argue that poetic talents are epistemologically valuable and ought not to be banished by philosophers.

See also INTUITION

RELATIONSHIPS

Our relations to each other are oblique and casual.

"Experience," *Essays,* Second Series (1844).

Almost all people descend to meet. All association must be a compromise, and, what is worst, the very flower and aroma of the flower of each of the beautiful natures disappears as they approach each other.

"Friendship," *Essays,* First Series (1841, repr. 1847).

Trust men, and they will be true to you; treat them greatly, and they will show themselves great, though they make an exception in your favor to all their rules of trade.

"Prudence," *Essays*, First Series (1841, repr. 1847).

RELATIVES

How shall a man escape from his ancestors, or draw off from his veins the black drop which he drew from his father's or mother's life?

"Fate," *The Conduct of Life* (1860).

See also INFLUENCES

In different hours, a man represents each of several of his ancestors, as if there were seven or eight of us rolled up in each man's skin,—seven or eight ancestors at least, and they constitute the variety of notes for that new piece of music which his life is.

"Fate," *The Conduct of Life* (1860).

A man is reputed to have thought and eloquence; he cannot, for all that, say a word to his cousin or his uncle. They accuse his silence with as much reason as they would blame the insignificance of a dial in the shade. In the sun it will mark the hour. Among those who enjoy his thought, he will regain his tongue.

"Friendship," *Essays*, First Series (1841, repr. 1847).

A thought for all those who have sulked through holidays with their extended families.

See also CONVERSATION

I cannot go to the houses of my nearest relatives, because I do not wish to be alone. Society exists by chemical affinity, and not otherwise.

"Society and Solitude," *Society and Solitude* (1870).

RELIGION

By it, is the universe made safe and habitable, not by science or power.

"The Divinity School Address," repr. in *The Portable Emerson*, ed. Carl Bode (1946, repr. 1981).

Address, July 15, 1838, delivered before the senior class in Divinity College, Cambridge.

See also SCIENCE

I knew a witty physician who found theology in the biliary duct, and used to affirm that if there was a disease in the liver, the man became a Calvinist, and if that organ was sound, he became a Unitarian.

"Experience," *Essays*, Second Series (1844).

Let us not deny it up and down. Providence has a wild, rough, incalculable road to its end, and it is of no use to try to whitewash its huge, mixed instrumentalities, or to dress up that terrific benefactor in a clean shirt and white neckcloth of a student of divinity.

"Fate," *The Conduct of Life* (1860).

See also NATURE

The foregoing generations beheld God and nature face to face; we, through their eyes. Why should not we also enjoy an original relation to the universe? Why should not we have a poetry and philosophy of insight and not of tradition, and a religion by revelation to us, and not the history of theirs?

Nature, Introduction, (1836, revised and repr. 1849).

The opening salvo of Emerson's book-length essay establishes the theme that will haunt most of his writings, namely the search for daily revelation unfettered by tradition or institutional strictures.

See also GOD

Therefore is nature ever the ally of Religion: lends her all her pomp and riches to the religious sentiment.

Nature, ch. 5, (1836, revised and repr. 1849).

See also NATURE

The reliance on authority measures the decline of religion, the withdrawal of the soul.

"The Over-Soul," *Essays*, First Series (1841, repr. 1847).

The religions of the world are the ejaculations of a few imaginative men.

"The Poet," *Essays*, Second Series (1844).

I like a church; I like a cowl;
I love a prophet of the soul;
And on my heart monastic aisles

Fall like sweet strains, or pensive smiles;
Yet not for all this faith can see
Would I that cowled churchman be.

"The Problem," *Poems* (1847).

Everywhere I am hindered of meeting God in my brother, because he has shut his own temple doors and recites fables merely of his brother's, or his brother's brother's God.

"Self-Reliance," *Essays*, First Series (1841, repr. 1847).

See also GOD

God builds his temple in the heart on the ruins of churches and religions.

"Worship," *The Conduct of Life* (1860).

Religion must always be a crab fruit: it cannot be grafted and keep its wild beauty.

"Worship," *The Conduct of Life* (1860).

There will be a new church founded on moral science, at first cold and naked, a babe in a manger again, the algebra and mathematics of ethical law, the church of men to come, without shams, or psaltery, or sackbut; but it will have heaven and earth for its beams and rafters; science for symbol and illustration; it will fast enough gather beauty, music, picture, poetry. Was never stoicism so stern and exigent as this shall be. It shall send man home to his central solitude, shame these social, supplicating manners, and make him know that much of the time he must have himself to his friend. He shall expect no cooperation, he shall walk with no companion.

"Worship," *The Conduct of Life* (1860).

An articulation of the later Emersonian vision of the evolution of religion. We must resist taking his version of individualism here as extreme isolationism. Just above this passage, Emerson speaks of a "voluntary obedience, a necessitated freedom." Again, Emerson struggles to find words and images for a connected individualism, where there are moments of inspiration and solitude that only bind the individual more thoroughly to the universe. He says "When his mind is illuminated, when his heart is kind, he throws himself joyfully into the sublime order, and does, with knowledge, what the stones do by structure." By adding a kind heart to this list, Emerson seeks to add human relationships to that sublime order to which the illuminated mind fuses in its moments of enlightenment. In other words, we go it alone, at times, only to become that much more connected to nature and humanity.

See also INDIVIDUALISM

REPUTATIONS

People forget that it is the eye that makes the horizon, and the rounding mind's eye which makes this or that man a type or representative of humanity with the name of hero or saint.

"Experience," *Essays*, Second Series (1844).

See also PERCEPTION

The great man knew not that he was great. It took a century or two for that fact to appear. What he did, he did because he must; it was the most natural thing in the world, and grew out of the circumstances of the moment. But now, every thing he did, even to the lifting of his finger or the eating of bread, looks large, all-related, and is called an institution.

"Spiritual Laws," *Essays*, First Series (1841, repr. 1847).

See also GREATNESS

RESPECT

I wish to speak with all respect of persons, but sometimes I must pinch myself to keep awake, and preserve the due decorum. They melt so fast into each other, that they are like grass and trees, and it needs an effort to treat them as individuals.

"Nominalist and Realist," *Essays*, Second Series (1844).

REVELATION

Is there any religion but this, to know, that, wherever in the wide desert of being, the holy sentiment we cherish has opened into a flower, it blooms for me? If none sees it, I see it; I am aware, if I alone, of the greatness of the fact. Whilst it blooms, I will keep sabbath or holy time, and suspend my gloom, and my folly and jokes.

"Character," *Essays*, Second Series (1844).

See also RELIGION

Eminent spiritualists shall have an incapacity of putting their act or word aloof from them, and seeing it bravely for the nothing it is. Beware of the man who says, "I am on the eve of a revelation."

"Culture," *The Conduct of Life* (1860).

Men have come to speak of the revelation as somewhat long ago given and done, as if God were dead. The injury to faith throttles the preacher; and the goodliest of institutions becomes an uncertain and inarticulate voice.

"The Divinity School Address," repr. in *The Portable Emerson*, ed. Carl Bode (1946, repr. 1981). Address, July 15, 1838, delivered before the senior class in Divinity College, Cambridge.

Another Nieztschean echo, except that Emerson is hypothetical and gentle ("as if God were dead"), as opposed to Zarathustra's resounding declaration that "God is dead."

See also GOD

For this communication is an influx of the Divine mind into our mind. It is an ebb of the individual rivulet before the flowing surges of the sea of life.

"The Over-Soul," *Essays*, First Series (1841, repr. 1847).

See also GOD

The soul answers never by words, but by the thing itself that is inquired after.

"The Over-Soul," *Essays*, First Series (1841, repr. 1847).

See also SOUL

ℛEWARDS

The reward of a thing well done, is to have done it.

"New England Reformers," *Essays*, Second Series (1844).

Lecture, March 3, 1844, in Amory Hall, Boston, Massachusetts.

SCHOOLS

Is it not manifest that our academic institutions should have a wider scope; that they should not be timid and keep the ruts of the last generation, but that wise men thinking for themselves and heartily seeking the good of mankind, and counting the cost of innovation, should dare to arouse the young to a just and heroic life; that the moral nature should be addressed in the school-room, and children should be treated as the high-born candidates of truth and virtue?

"Education," *Lectures and Biographical Sketches* (1883, repr. 1904).

See also EDUCATION

SCIENCE

But what is classification but the perceiving that these objects are not chaotic, and are not foreign, but have a law which is also the law of the human mind?

"The American Scholar," repr. in *Emerson: Essays and Lectures*, ed. Joel Porte (1983).

Oration, August 31, 1837, delivered before the Phi Beta Kappa Society, Cambridge, Massachusetts.

See also MIND, THE

Science is nothing but the finding of analogy, identity, in the most remote parts.

"The American Scholar," repr. in *Emerson: Essays and Lectures*, ed. Joel Porte (1983).

Oration, August 31, 1837, delivered before the Phi Beta Kappa Society, Cambridge, Massachusetts.

Science in England, in America, is jealous of theory, hates the name of love and moral purpose. There's revenge for this humanity. What manner of man does science make? The boy is not attracted. He says, I do not wish to be such a kind of man as my professor is.

"Beauty," *The Conduct of Life* (1860).

See also EDUCATION

The human heart concerns us more than the poring into microscopes, and is larger than can be measured by the pompous figures of the astronomer.

"Beauty," *The Conduct of Life* (1860).

The motive of science was the extension of man, on all sides, into Nature, till his hands should touch the stars, his eyes see through the earth, his ears understand the language of beast and bird, and the sense of the wind;

and, through his sympathy, heaven and earth should talk with him. But that is not our science.

"Beauty," *The Conduct of Life* (1860).

Our eyes
Are armed, but we are strangers to the stars,
And strangers to the mystic beast and bird,
And strangers to the plant and to the mine.

"Blight," *Poems* (1847).

See also CONNECTEDNESS

We may climb into the thin and cold realm of pure geometry and lifeless science, or sink into that of sensation. Between these extremes is the equator of life, of thought, or spirit, or poetry,—a narrow belt.

"Experience," *Essays,* Second Series (1844).

People seem sheathed in their tough organization.

"Fate," *The Conduct of Life* (1860).

It is the last lesson of modern science, that the highest simplicity of structure is produced, not by few elements, but by the highest complexity.

"Goethe; or, the Writer," *Representative Men* (1850).

Empirical science is apt to cloud the sight, and, by the very knowledge of functions and processes, to bereave the student of the manly contemplation of the whole.

Nature, ch. 8, (1836, revised and repr. 1849).

It is, in both cases, that a spiritual life has been imparted to nature; that the solid seeming block of matter has been pervaded and dissolved by a thought; that this feeble human being has penetrated the vast masses of nature with an informing soul, and recognised itself in their harmony, that is, seized their law. In physics, when this is attained, the memory disburthens itself of its cumbrous catalogues of particulars, and carries centuries of observation in a single formula.

Nature, ch. 6, (1836, revised and repr. 1849).

The axioms of physics translate the laws of ethics. Thus, "the whole is greater than its part;" "reaction is equal to action;" "the smallest weight may be made to lift the greatest, the difference of weight being compensated by time;" and many the like propositions, which have an ethical as well as physical sense. These propositions have a much more extensive and universal sense when applied to human life, than when confined to technical use.

Nature, ch. 4, (1836, revised and repr. 1849).

To the intelligent, nature converts itself into a vast promise, and will not be rashly explained. Her secret is untold. Many and many an Oedipus arrives: he has the whole mystery teeming in his brain. Alas! the same sorcery has spoiled his skill; no syllable can he shape on his lips.

"Nature," *Essays,* Second Series (1844).

The terrible tabulation of the French statists brings every piece of whim and humor to be reducible also to exact numerical ratios. If one man in twenty thousand, or in thirty thousand, eats shoes, or marries his grandmother, then, in every twenty thousand, or thirty thousand, is found one man who eats shoes, or marries his grandmother.

"Swedenborg; or, the Mystic," *Representative Men* (1850).

Emerson's point is that statistics don't tell good stories, nor do they honor the place of whim in the universe. They render the world uninteresting.

*S*CULPTURE

When I have seen fine statues, and afterwards enter a public assembly, I understand well what he meant who said, "When I have been reading Homer, all men look like giants."

"Art," *Essays,* First Series (1841, repr. 1847).

The god or hero of the sculptor is always represented in a transition *from* that which is representable to the senses, *to* that which is not.

"Love," *Essays,* First Series (1841, repr. 1847).

*S*ELF

The world is nothing, the man is all; in yourself is the law of all nature, and you know not yet how a globule of sap ascends; in yourself slumbers the whole of Reason; it is for you to know all; it is for you to dare all.

"The American Scholar," repr. In *Emerson: Essays and Lectures*, ed. Joel Porte (1983).

Oration, August 31, 1837, delivered before the Phi Beta Kappa Society, Cambridge, Massachusetts.

The covetousness or the malignity, which saddens me, when I ascribe it to society, is my own. I am environed by my self.

"Character," *Essays*, Second Series (1844).

Every man supposes himself not to be fully understood; and if there is any truth in him, if he rests at last on the divine soul, I see not how it could be otherwise. The last chamber, the last closet, he must feel was never opened; there is always a residuum unknown, unanalyzable. That is, every man believes that he has greater possibility.

"Circles," *Essays*, First Series (1841, repr. 1847).

So all that is said of the wise man by Stoic or Oriental or modern essayist, describes to each reader his own idea, describes his unattained but attainable self.

"History," *Essays*, First Series (1841, repr. 1847).

Here Emerson links notions of self-realization and reading, and in so doing, summarizes his philosophy of education. The philosopher Stanley Cavell has characterized this idea as "nextness," meaning that Emerson is continually in search of that perfect self which lies just next to our present selves and toward which we turn to become. Finding the right representative, whether it be a person or a text, is essential for this Emersonian type of growth.

See also READING

Do not you see that every misfortune is misconduct; that every honour is desert; that every effort is an insolence of your own? . . . You carry your fortune in your own hand.

The Journals and Miscellaneous Notebooks of Ralph Waldo Emerson, vol. 3, (1960–1978).

We do not yet possess ourselves, and we know at the same time that we are much more.

"The Over-Soul," *Essays*, First Series (1841, repr. 1847).

See also HUMAN DEVELOPMENT

Trust thyself: every heart vibrates to that iron string.

"Self-Reliance," *Essays*, First Series (1841, repr. 1847).

We but half express ourselves, and are ashamed of that divine idea which each of us represents.

"Self-Reliance," *Essays*, First Series (1841, repr. 1847).

I—this thought which is called I—is the mould into which the world is poured like melted wax.

"The Transcendentalist," repr. in *The Portable Emerson*, ed. Carl Bode (1946, repr. 1981).

Compare this with the wax motif in Descartes's *Meditations*.

SILENCE

Good as is discourse, silence is better, and shames it. The length of the discourse indicates the distance of thought betwixt the speaker and the hearer. If they were at a perfect understanding in any part, no words would be necessary thereon. If at one in all parts, no words would be suffered.

"Circles," *Essays*, First Series (1841, repr. 1847).

See also UNDERSTANDING

Silence is a solvent that destroys personality, and gives us leave to be great and universal.

"Intellect," *Essays*, First Series (1841, repr. 1847).

Ye taught my lips a single speech,
And a thousand silences.

"Merops," *Poems* (1847).

See also LANGUAGE

Speech is better than silence; silence is better than speech.

"Nominalist and Realist," *Essays*, Second Series (1844).

The path of things is silent. Will they suffer a speaker to go with them?

"The Poet," *Essays*, Second Series (1844).

See also LANGUAGE

But real action is in silent moments. The epochs of our life are not in the visible facts of our choice of a calling, our marriage, our acquisition of an office, and the like, but in a silent thought by the way-side as we walk; in a thought which revises our entire manner of life, and says,—"Thus hast thou done, but it were better thus."

"Spiritual Laws," *Essays*, First Series (1841, repr. 1847).

See also THINKING AND THOUGHT

SIMPLICITY

In rhetoric, this art of omission is a chief secret of power, and, in general, it is proof of high culture to say the greatest matters in the simplest way.

"Beauty," *The Conduct of Life* (1860).

Let us learn to live coarsely, dress plainly, and lie hard. The least habit of dominion over the palate has certain good effects not easily estimated.

"Culture," *The Conduct of Life* (1860).

Who liveth by the ragged pine
Foundeth a heroic line;
Who liveth in the palace hall
Waneth fast and spendeth all.

"Woodnotes II," *Poems* (1847).

See also WEALTH AND THE WEALTHY

SKEPTICISM

I take this evanescence and lubricity of all objects, which lets them slip through our fingers then when we clutch hardest, to be the most un-handsome part of our condition.

"Experience," *Essays*, Second Series (1844).

Stanley Cavell has commented on this passage and the image of "unhandsomeness," which he links as much to the pun on "hand" and its relation to grasping, that is, understanding, as to a lack of beauty and grace.

See also KNOWLEDGE

Life itself is a bubble and a skepticism, and a sleep within sleep.

"Experience," *Essays, Second Series* (1844).

God never jests with us, and will not compromise the end of nature, by permitting any inconsequence in its procession.

Nature, ch. 6, (1836, revised and repr. 1849).

A reference to Descartes and his argument that God would not deceive us.

See also GOD

In my utter impotence to test the authenticity of the report of my senses, to know whether the impressions they make on me correspond with outlying objects, what difference does it make, whether Orion is up there in heaven, or some god paints the image in the firmament of the soul?

Nature, ch. 6, (1836, revised and repr. 1849).

See also KNOWLEDGE

S*LAVERY*

America is not civil, whilst Africa is barbarous.

"Address Delivered in Concord on the Anniversary of the Emancipation of the Negroes in the British West Indies, August 1, 1844," *Miscellanies* (1883, repr. 1904).

Edward Emerson notes that "Boston Hymn" sings a similar sentiment. Emerson is not commenting on the nature of African civilization, but noting the barbarity of the slave trade on its shores.

If any mention was made of homicide, madness, adultery, and intolerable tortures, we would let the church-bells ring louder, the church-organ swell its peal and drown the hideous sound. The sugar they raised was excellent: nobody tasted blood in it.

"Address Delivered in Concord on the Anniversary of the Emancipation of the Negroes in the British West Indies, August 1, 1844," *Miscellanies* (1883, repr. 1904).

If there be any man who thinks the ruin of a race of men a small matter, compared with the last decoration and completions of his own comfort,—who would not so much as part with his ice-cream, to save them from rapine and manacles, I think I must not hesitate to satisfy that man that also his cream and vanilla are safer and cheaper by placing the negro nation on a fair footing than by robbing them.

"Address Delivered in Concord on the Anniversary of the Emancipation of the Negroes in the British West Indies, August 1, 1844," *Miscellanies* (1883, repr. 1904).

Slavery is no scholar, no improver; it does not love the whistle of the railroad; it does not love the newspaper, the mail-bag, a college, a book or a preacher who has the absurd whim of saying what he thinks; it does not increase the white population; it does not improve the soil; everything goes to decay.

"Address Delivered in Concord on the Anniversary of the Emancipation of the Negroes in the British West Indies, August 1, 1844," *Miscellanies* (1883, repr. 1904).

The blood is moral: the blood is anti-slavery: it runs cold in the veins: the stomach rises with disgust, and curses slavery.

"Address Delivered in Concord on the Anniversary of the Emancipation of the Negroes in the British West Indies, August 1, 1844," *Miscellanies* (1883, repr. 1904).

The subject is said to have the property of making dull men eloquent.

"Address Delivered in Concord on the Anniversary of the Emancipation of the Negroes in the British West Indies, August 1, 1844," *Miscellanies* (1883, repr. 1904).

Give the slave the least elevation of religious sentiment, and he is not slave: you are the slave: he not only in his humility feels his superiority, feels that much deplored condition of his to be a fading trifle, but he makes you feel it too. He is the master.

"Introductory Lecture on the Times," *Nature, Addresses, and Lectures* (1849). Speech, December 2, 1841, at the Masonic Temple, Boston, Massachusetts.

Although this quotation contains obvious Hegelian themes, Emerson would not begin a serious study of Hegel for another eight years.

*S*OCIETY

Society is frivolous, and shreds its day into scraps, its conversation into ceremonies and escapes.

"Character," *Essays,* Second Series (1844).

The virtues of society are vices of the saint.

"Circles," *Essays,* First Series (1841, repr. 1847).

See also VIRTUE

Fine society is only a self-protection against the vulgarities of the street and tavern.

"Considerations by the Way," *The Conduct of Life* (1860).

The longer we live the more we must endure the elementary existence of men and women; and every brave heart must treat society as a child, and never allow it to dictate.

"Culture," *The Conduct of Life* (1860).

Society always consists, in greatest part, of young and foolish persons. The old, who have seen through the hypocrisy of the courts and statesmen, die, and leave no wisdom to their sons. They believe their own newspaper, as their fathers did at their age.

"Politics," *Essays,* Second Series (1844).

See also AGE AND AGING

Society everywhere is in conspiracy against the manhood of every one of its members. Society is a joint-stock company, in which the members agree, for the better securing of his bread to each shareholder, to surrender the liberty and culture of the eater.

"Self-Reliance," *Essays,* First Series (1841, repr. 1847).

Society is a masked ball, where everyone hides his real character, and reveals it by hiding.

"Worship," *The Conduct of Life* (1860).

See also SELF

SOLITUDE

Think me not unkind and rude
That I walk alone in grove and glen;
I go to the god of the wood
To fetch his word to men.

"The Apology," *Poems* (1847).

Keep the town for occasions, but the habits should be formed in retirement.

"Culture," *The Conduct of Life* (1860).

Solitude, the safeguard of mediocrity, is to genius, the stern friend, the cold, obscure shelter where moult the wings which will bear it farther than suns and stars.

"Culture," *The Conduct of Life* (1860).

I am grown by sympathy a little eager and sentimental, but leave me alone, and I should relish every hour and what it brought me, the pot-luck of the day, as heartily as the oldest gossip in the bar-room.

"Experience," *Essays*, Second Series (1844).

I am not solitary whilst I read and write, though nobody is with me. But if a man would be alone, let him look at the stars.

Nature, ch. 1, (1836, revised and repr. 1849).

See also ASTRONOMY

But your isolation must not be mechanical, but spiritual, that is, must be elevation.

"Self-Reliance," *Essays*, First Series (1841, repr. 1847).

It is easy in the world to live after the world's opinion; it is easy in solitude to live after our own; but the great man is he who in the midst of a crowd keeps with perfect sweetness the independence of solitude.

"Self-Reliance," *Essays*, First Series (1841, repr. 1847).

See also INDIVIDUALISM

It is better to be alone than in bad company.

"The Transcendentalist," repr. in *The Portable Emerson*, ed. Carl Bode (1946, repr. 1981).

Speech, January 1842, at the Masonic Temple in Boston, repr. in *The Dial* (1843) and *Nature, Addresses, and Lectures* (1849).

Society, to be sure, does not like this very well; it saith, Whoso goes to walk alone, accuses the whole world; he declares all to be unfit to be his companions; it is very uncivil, nay, insulting; Society will retaliate.

"The Transcendentalist," repr. in *The Portable Emerson*, ed. Carl Bode (1946, repr. 1981).

Speech, January 1842, at the Masonic Temple in Boston, repr. in *The Dial* (1843) and *Nature, Addresses, and Lectures* (1849).

See also SOCIETY

Whoso walketh in solitude,
And inhabiteth the wood,
Choosing light, wave, rock, and bird,

Before the money-loving herd,
Into that forester shall pass,
From these companions, power and grace.

"Woodnotes II," *Poems* (1847).

SOUL

There is no great and no small
To the Soul that maketh all.

"History," *Essays*, First Series (1841, repr. 1847).

When he has seen, that it is not his, nor any man's, but it is the soul which made the world, and that it is all accessible to him, he will know that he, as its minister, may rightfully hold all things subordinate and answerable to it.

"Literary Ethics," *Nature, Addresses, and Lectures* (1849).

"He" is the Emersonian scholar. This quotation is interesting in that in one sentence Emerson juxtaposes the individual mind, the universe, and the universal soul. It is these three elements in dialectical dance that constitute Emerson's concept of connected individualism.

See also INDIVIDUALISM

All goes to show that the soul in man is not an organ, but animates and exercises all the organs; is not a function, like the power of memory, of calculation, of comparison, but uses these as hands and feet; is not a faculty, but a light, is not the intellect or the will, but the master of the intellect and the will; is the background of our being, in which they lie,— an immensity not possessed and that cannot be possessed.

"The Over-Soul," *Essays*, First Series (1841, repr. 1847).

The soul circumscribes all things.

"The Over-Soul," *Essays*, First Series (1841, repr. 1847).

The soul knows only the soul; the web of events is the flowing robe in which she is clothed.

"The Over-Soul," *Essays*, First Series (1841, repr. 1847).

The universe is the externisation of the soul. Wherever the life is, that bursts into appearance around it. Our science is sensual, and therefore superficial. The earth, and the heavenly bodies, physics, and chemistry, we sensually treat, as if they were self-existent; but these are the retinue of that Being we have.

"The Poet," *Essays,* Second Series (1844).

See also SCIENCE

If you believe in the soul, do not clutch at sensual sweetness before it is ripe on the slow tree of cause and effect.

"Prudence," *Essays,* First Series (1841, repr. 1847).

See also SPIRITUALITY/PRAYER

The Soul rules over matter. Matter may pass away like a mote in the sunbeam, may be absorbed into the immensity of God, as a mist is absorbed into the heat of the Sun—but the soul is the kingdom of God, the abode of love, of truth, of virtue.

Quoted in the Notes to "The Lord's Supper," *Miscellanies* (1883, repr. 1904).

Journal entry, March, 1831.

*S*PIRITUALITY

Moons are no more bounds to spiritual power than bat-balls.

"Circles," *Essays,* First Series (1841, repr. 1847).

Emerson is speaking here about the illusion of permanence and connecting the idea of flux to the non-empirical realm of spirituality. The notion is that spiritual power blooms in the context of change and mutability. If all were permanently stable, Emerson argues, the sacred would not be able to appear in nature. Moons in the solar system and earthly balls dancing off the end of a bat represent the spectrum of possibility in the universe.

Whilst we converse with what is above us, we do not grow old, but grow young.

"Circles," *Essays,* First Series (1841, repr. 1847).

See also RELIGION

There is no doctrine of the Reason which will bear to be taught by the Understanding.

"The Divinity School Address," repr. in *The Portable Emerson,* ed. Carl Bode (1946, repr. 1981). Address, July 15, 1838, delivered before the senior class in Divinity College, Cambridge.

Here, Emerson appropriates aspects of Kant's terminology. For Kant, the "understanding" is that mental capacity tied to sense data, whereas "reason" is the cognitive faculty with which we can conceive of ideal qualities beyond sensual data e.g., freedom or God. It should be noted that Kant's definition for "reason" expands at different points in his writings.

See also KNOWLEDGE

The use of natural history is to give us aid in supernatural history: the use of the outer creation, to give us language for the beings and changes of the inward creation.

Nature, ch. 4, (1836, revised and repr. 1849).

See also NATURE

The soul lets no man go without some visitations and holy-days of a diviner presence.

"New England Reformers," *Essays*, Second Series (1844).

Lecture, March 3, 1844, in Amory Hall, Boston, Massachusetts.

See also GOD

For, rightly, every man is a channel through which heaven floweth, and, whilst I fancied I was criticising him, I was censuring or rather terminating my own soul.

"Nominalist and Realist," *Essays*, Second Series (1844).

See also HEAVEN

What we commonly call man, the eating, drinking, planting, counting man, does not, as we know him, represent himself, but misrepresents himself. Him we do not respect, but the soul, whose organ he is, would he let it appear through his action, would make our knees bend.

"The Over-Soul," *Essays*, First Series (1841, repr. 1847).

See also SOUL

We have had many harbingers and forerunners; but of a purely spiritual life, history has afforded no example. I mean we have yet no man who has leaned entirely on his character, and eaten angels' food; who, trusting to his sentiments, found life made of miracles; who, working for universal aims, found himself fed, he knew not how; clothed, sheltered, and weaponed, he knew not how, and yet it was done by his own hands.

"The Transcendentalist," repr. in *The Portable Emerson*, ed. Carl Bode (1946, repr. 1981).

Speech, January 1842, at the Masonic Temple in Boston, repr. in *The Dial* (1843) and *Nature, Addresses, and Lectures* (1849).

In our definitions, we grope after the spiritual by describing it as invisible. The true meaning of spiritual is real; that law which executes itself, which works without means, and which cannot be conceived as not existing.

"Worship," *The Conduct of Life* (1860).

See also GOD

*S*TUDENTS

Is not, indeed, every man a student, and do not all things exist for the student's behoof?

"The American Scholar," repr. in *Emerson: Essays and Lectures*, ed. Joel Porte (1983).

Oration, August 31, 1837, delivered before the Phi Beta Kappa Society, Cambridge, Massachusetts.

Meek young men grow up in libraries, believing it their duty to accept the views, which Cicero, which Locke, which Bacon, have given, forgetful that Cicero, Locke, and Bacon were only young men in libraries, when they wrote these books.

"The American Scholar," repr. in *Emerson: Essays and Lectures*, ed. Joel Porte (1983).

Oration, August 31, 1837, delivered before the Phi Beta Kappa Society, Cambridge, Massachusetts.

See also KNOWLEDGE

*S*UCCESS

That you are fair or wise is vain,
Or strong, or rich, or generous;
You must have also the untaught strain
That sheds beauty on the rose.

"Fate," *Poems* (1847).

See also BEAUTY

Sanity consists in not being subdued by your means. Fancy prices are paid for position, and for the culture of talent, but to the grand interests, superficial success is of no account.

"Considerations by the Way," *The Conduct of Life* (1860).

All successful men have agreed in one thing,—they were causationists. They believed that things went not by luck, but by law; that there was not a weak or a cracked link in the chain that joins the first and last of things.

"Power," *The Conduct of Life* (1860).

Every true man is a cause, a country, and an age; requires infinite spaces and numbers and time fully to accomplish his design;—and posterity seem to follow his steps as a train of clients.

"Self-Reliance," *Essays*, First Series (1841, repr. 1847).

The secret of success lies never in the amount of money, but in the relation of income to outgo.

"Wealth," *The Conduct of Life* (1860).

I look on that man as happy, who, when there is question of success, looks into his work for a reply, not into the market, not into opinion, not into patronage.

"Worship," *The Conduct of Life* (1860).

See also WORK

SUFFERING

Drudgery, calamity, exasperation, want, are instructors in eloquence and wisdom.

"The American Scholar," repr. In *Emerson: Essays and Lectures*, ed. Joel Porte (1983).

Oration, August 31, 1837, delivered before the Phi Beta Kappa Society, Cambridge, Massachusetts.

See also WISDOM

Why should I keep holiday
When other men have none?
Why but because, when these are gay,
I sit and mourn alone.

"Compensation," *Poems* (1847).

I grieve that grief can teach me nothing, nor carry me one step into real nature.

"Experience," *Essays*, Second Series (1844).

There are moods in which we court suffering, in the hope that here, at least, we shall find reality, sharp peaks and edges of truth. But it turns out to be scene-painting and counterfeit. The only thing grief has taught me, is to know how shallow it is.

"Experience," *Essays*, Second Series (1844).

See also PAIN

What opium is instilled into all disaster? It shows formidable as we approach it, but there is at last no rough rasping friction, but the most slippery sliding surfaces. We fall soft on a thought.

"Experience," *Essays*, Second Series (1844).

Emerson's point is that experience is such a difficult thing for us to get hold of and to understand, that even the most painful and difficult times seem to elude our full ability to truly know and grasp the succeeding moments of time.

See also PAIN

He has seen but half the universe who never has been shown the house of pain.

The Journals of Ralph Waldo Emerson, vol. 2, ed. Edward W. Emerson (1909–1914).

All loss, all pain, is particular; the universe remains to the heart unhurt.

"Spiritual Laws," *Essays*, First Series (1841, repr. 1847).

See also UNIVERSE, THE

*T*EACHERS AND TEACHING

The spirit only can teach. Not any profane man, not any sensual, not any liar, not any slave can teach, but only he can give, who has; he only can create, who is. The man on whom the soul descends, through whom the soul speaks, alone can teach. Courage, piety, love, wisdom, can teach; and every man can open his door to these angels, and they shall bring him the gift of tongues. But the man who aims to speak as books enable, as synods use, as the fashion guides, and as interest commands, babbles. Let him hush.

"The Divinity School Address," repr. in *The Portable Emerson*, ed. Carl Bode (1946, repr. 1981). Address, July 15, 1838, delivered before the senior class in Divinity College, Cambridge.

As every medical student upon graduation must take the Hippocratic oath, perhaps we should require every commencing teacher to recite this passage.

See also EDUCATION

Teaching is the perpetual end and office of all things. Teaching, instruction is the main design that shines through the sky and earth.

Quoted in Robert D. Richardson, Jr., *Emerson: The Mind on Fire*, ch. 25, (1995).

If a teacher have any opinion which he wishes to conceal, his pupils will become as fully indoctrinated into that as into any which he publishes.

"Spiritual Laws," *Essays*, First Series (1841, repr. 1847).

See also EDUCATION

There is no teaching until the pupil is brought into the same state or principle in which you are; a transfusion takes place; he is you, and you are he; then is a teaching; and by no unfriendly chance or bad company can he ever lose the benefit.

"Spiritual Laws," *Essays*, First Series (1841, repr. 1847).

See also EDUCATION

*T*HINKING AND THOUGHT

Generalization is always a new influx of divinity into the mind. Hence the thrill that attends it.

"Circles," *Essays*, First Series (1841, repr. 1847).

Do not craze yourself with thinking, but go about your business anywhere.

"Experience," *Essays*, Second Series (1844).

So far as man thinks, he is free.

"Fate," *The Conduct of Life* (1860).

Thought dissolves the material universe by carrying the mind up into a sphere where all is plastic.

"Fate," *The Conduct of Life* (1860).

Our thinking is a pious reception.

"Intellect," *Essays*, First Series (1841, repr. 1847).

This might serve as the motto for all of Emerson's epistemology. His notion of the mind is not that of a grasping tool. Instead, to think is to receive, as Emerson stated early on in his July 29, 1831 journal entry. Hence thought is a mode and a mood of revelation. In this same essay, Emerson goes on to explain that we have little control over what we think and must suffer the rolling tides of our cognition.

See also MIND, THE

What is the hardest task in the world? To think.

"Intellect," *Essays, First Series* (1841, repr. 1847).

In the uttermost meaning of the words, thought is devout, and devotion is thought. Deep calls unto deep.

Nature, ch. 8, (1836, revised and repr. 1849).

See also WORSHIP

Thoughts come into our minds by avenues which we never left open, and thoughts go out of our minds through avenues which we never voluntarily opened.

"The Over-Soul," *Essays, First Series* (1841, repr. 1847).

See also WILL

The people fancy they hate poetry, and they are all poets and mystics.

"The Poet," *Essays: Second Series* (1844).

Emerson refers to the fact that our everyday life is filled with symbols, emblems, and rituals. The tone here is reminiscent of Hegel's essay, "Who Thinks Abstractly?" where he argues that it is the "uneducated" who think the most abstractly, for they do not take the time to fill out the details of their experience, but just see things in terms of bald labels.

See also POETRY AND POETS

In every work of genius we recognize our own rejected thoughts; they come back to us with a certain alienated majesty.

"Self-Reliance," *Essays, First Series* (1841, repr. 1847).

To think is to act.

"Spiritual Laws," *Essays, First Series* (1841, repr. 1847).

See also ACTION

*T*IME

Illusion, Temperament, Succession, Surface, Surprise, Reality, Subjectiveness,—these are the threads on the loom of time, these are the lords of life.

"Experience," *Essays,* Second Series (1844).

See also REALITY AND REALISM

So much of our time is preparation, so much is routine, and so much retrospect, that the pith of each man's genius contracts itself to a very few hours.

"Experience," *Essays,* Second Series (1844).

See also LIFE

There is a relation between the hours of our life and the centuries of time. As the air I breathe is drawn from the great repositories of nature, as the light on my book is yielded by a star a hundred millions of miles distant, as the poise of my body depends on the equilibrium of centrifugal and centripetal forces, so the hours should be instructed by the ages and the ages explained by the hours.

"History," *Essays,* First Series (1841, repr. 1847).

For the time of towns is tolled from the world by funereal chimes, but in nature the universal hours are counted by succeeding tribes of animals and plants, and by growth of joy on joy.

"The Poet," *Essays,* Second Series (1844).

A moment is a concentrated eternity.

Quoted in Robert D. Richardson, Jr., *Emerson: The Mind on Fire,* ch. 41, (1995).

TRAVELING AND TRAVELERS

For the most part, only the light characters travel. Who are you that have no task to keep you at home?

"Culture," *The Conduct of Life* (1860).

I am not much an advocate for traveling, and I observe that men run away to other countries, because they are not good in their own, and run back to their own, because they pass for nothing in the new places.

"Culture," *The Conduct of Life* (1860).

No doubt, to a man of sense, travel offers advantages. As many languages as he has, as many friends, as many arts and trades, so many times is he a man. A foreign country is a point of comparison, wherefrom to judge his own.

"Culture," *The Conduct of Life* (1860).

Everything good is on the highway.

"Experience," *Essays*, Second Series (1844).

Emerson repeats this dictum twice in the essay, articulating the notion that it is not where you end up that is so important, but the quality of the experience of getting there. In other words, it's not the race, it's the ride.

See also HIGHWAYS

Do not require a description of the countries towards which you sail. The description does not describe them to you, and to-morrow you arrive there, and know them by inhabiting them.

"The Over-Soul," *Essays*, First Series (1841).

It is for want of self-culture that the superstition of Travelling, whose idols are Italy, England, Egypt, retains its fascination for all educated Americans.

"Self-Reliance," *Essays*, First Series (1841, repr. 1847).

The soul is no traveler; the wise man stays at home, and when his necessities, his duties, on any occasion call him from his house, or into foreign lands, he is at home still and shall make men sensible by the expression of his countenance that he goes, the missionary of wisdom and virtue, and visits cities and men like a sovereign and not like an interloper or a valet.

"Self-Reliance," *Essays*, First Series (1841, repr. 1847).

Traveling is a fool's paradise. Our first journeys discover to us the indifference of places. At home I dream that at Naples, at Rome, I can be intoxicated with beauty and lose my sadness. I pack my trunk, embrace my friends, embark on the sea, and at last wake up in Naples, and there beside me is the stern fact, the sad self, unrelenting, identical, that I fled from.

"Self-Reliance," *Essays*, First Series (1841, repr. 1847).

*T*RUTH

Let him not quit his belief that a popgun is a popgun, though the ancient and honorable of the earth affirm it to be the crack of doom.

"The American Scholar," repr. In *Emerson: Essays and Lectures*, ed. Joel Porte (1983).

The popgun metaphor is a wonderful imagistic summary of Emerson's confidence in the authentic individual being able to access truth. As always, we should be cautioned against interpreting

Emerson as a radical individualist or separatist. The notion is that by staying true to our instincts we may enter a more universal community. He says a bit later in "The American Scholar": "He then learns, that in going down into the secrets of his own mind, he has descended into the secrets of all minds."

See also CONFORMITY

But speak the truth, and all nature and all spirits help you with unexpected furtherance. Speak the truth, and all things alive or brute are vouchers, and the very roots of the grass underground there do seem to stir and move to bear you witness.

"The Divinity School Address," repr. in *The Portable Emerson,* ed. Carl Bode (1946, repr. 1981).

Address, July 15, 1838, delivered before the senior class in Divinity College, Cambridge.

And one may say boldly that no man has a right perception of any truth who has not been reacted on by it so as to be ready to be its martyr.

"Fate," *The Conduct of Life* (1860).

I cannot often enough say, that a man is only a relative and representative nature. Each is a hint of the truth, but far enough from being that truth, which yet he quite newly and inevitably suggests to us. If I seek it in him, I shall not find it.

"Nominalist and Realist," *Essays,* Second Series (1844).

We know truth when we see it, from opinion, as we know when we are awake that we are awake.

"The Over-Soul," *Essays,* First Series (1841, repr. 1847).

Every man finds a sanction for his simplest claims and deeds, in decisions of his own mind, which he calls Truth and Holiness.

"Politics," *Essays,* Second Series (1844).

Every violation of truth is not only a sort of suicide in the liar, but is a stab at the health of human society.

"Prudence," *Essays,* First Series (1841, repr. 1847).

Truth has not single victories; all things are its organs,—not only dust and stones, but errors and lies.

"Spiritual Laws," *Essays,* First Series (1841, repr. 1847).

Understanding

The simplest words,—we do not know what they mean except when we love and aspire.

"Circles," *Essays*, First Series (1841, repr. 1847).

See also SIMPLICITY

But every insight from this realm of thought is felt as initial, and promises a sequel. I do not make it; I arrive there, and behold what was there already. I make! O no! I clap my hands in infantine joy and amazement, before the first opening to me of this august magnificence, old with the love and homage of innumerable ages, young with the life of life, the sunbright Mecca of the desert.

"Experience," *Essays*, Second Series (1844).

My companion assumes to know my mood and habit of thought, and we go on from explanation to explanation, until all is said that words can, and we leave matters just as they were at first, because of that vicious assumption.

"Nominalist and Realist," *Essays*, Second Series (1844).

With his emphasis on the boundaries of explanation and the limits of language, Emerson strikes a distinctly Wittgensteinian tone here.

United States

Our day of dependence, our long apprenticeship to the learning of other lands, draws to a close. The millions, that around us are rushing into life, cannot always be fed on the sere remains of foreign harvests.

"The American Scholar," repr. in *Emerson: Essays and Lectures*, ed. Joel Porte (1983).

Oration, August 31, 1837, delivered before the Phi Beta Kappa Society, Cambridge, Massachusetts.

See also INDEPENDENCE

The mind of this country, taught to aim at low objects, eats upon itself.

"The American Scholar," repr. in *Emerson: Essays and Lectures*, ed. Joel Porte (1983).

Oration, August 31, 1837, delivered before the Phi Beta Kappa Society, Cambridge, Massachusetts.

Young men of the fairest promise, who begin life upon our shores, inflated by the mountain winds, shined upon by all the stars of God, find the earth below not in unison with these,—but are hindered from action by the disgust which the principles on which business is managed inspire, and turn drudges, or die of disgust,—some of them suicides.

"The American Scholar," repr. in *Emerson: Essays and Lectures,* ed. Joel Porte (1983).

Oration, August 31, 1837, delivered before the Phi Beta Kappa Society, Cambridge, Massachusetts.

See also YOUTH

In America, the geography is sublime, but the men are not: the inventions are excellent, but the inventors one is sometimes ashamed of.

"Considerations by the Way," *The Conduct of Life* (1860).

Alas for America as I must so often say, the ungirt, the diffuse, the profuse, procumbent, one wide ground juniper, out of which no cedar, no oak will rear up a mast to the clouds! It all runs to leaves, to suckers, to tendrils, to miscellany. The air is loaded with poppy, with imbecility, with dispersion, & sloth.

Emerson in His Journals, June 1847, ed. Joel Porte (1982).

American mind a wilderness of opportunities.

Emerson in His Journals, June 1847, ed. Joel Porte (1982).

I am ready to die out of nature, and be born again into this new yet unapproachable America I have found in the West.

"Experience," *Essays,* Second Series (1844).

See also REBIRTH

Yet America is a poem in our eyes; its ample geography dazzles the imagination, and it will not wait long for metres.

"The Poet," *Essays,* Second Series (1844).

Great country, diminutive minds. America is formless, has no terrible and no beautiful condensation.

Quoted in Harold Bloom, *The American Religion,* (1992).

Journal entry, June 1847.

From Washington, proverbially "the city of distances," through all its cities, states, and territories, it is a country of beginnings, of projects, of designs, and expectations.

"The Young American," *Nature, Addresses, and Lectures* (1849).

Speech, February 7, 1844, the Mercantile Library Association, Boston, Massachusetts.

One thing is plain for all men of common sense and common conscience, that here, here in America, is the home of man. After all the deductions which are to be made of for our pitiful politics, which stake every gravest national question on the silly die, whether James or whether Jonathan shall sit in the chair and hold the purse; after all the deduction is made for our frivolities and insanities, there still remains an organic simplicity and liberty, which, when it loses its balance, redresses itself presently, which offers opportunity to the human mind not known in any other region.

"The Young American," *Nature, Addresses, and Lectures* (1849). Speech, February 7, 1844, the Mercantile Library Association, Boston, Massachusetts.

The reference to "common sense" can be taken as a reference to Thomas Paine's famous pamphlet, written in January 1776, which argued that the American colonies had outgrown the British and ought to break free. In a similar fashion, Emerson in this speech and elsewhere argues for a second, cultural American revolution where the East Coast ought to break free from English letters, literature and customs and light out for the Western territories toward a more spiritually authentic original America.

U*NITY*

Underneath the inharmonious and trivial particulars, is a musical perfection, the Ideal journeying always with us, the heaven without rent or seam.

"Experience," *Essays*, Second Series (1844).

See also IDEALISM

Let us build altars to the Blessed Unity which holds nature and souls in perfect solution, and compels every atom to serve an universal end.

"Fate," *The Conduct of Life* (1860).

The reason why the world lacks unity, and lies broken and in heaps, is, because man is disunited with himself.

Nature, ch. 8, (1836, revised and repr. 1849).

UNIVERSITIES AND COLLEGES

Colleges, in like manner, have their indispensable office,—to teach elements. But they can only highly serve us, when they aim not to drill, but to create; when they gather from far every ray of various genius to their hospitable halls, and, by the concentrated fires, set the hearts of their youth on flame.

"The American Scholar," repr. in *Emerson: Essays and Lectures*, ed. Joel Porte (1983).

Oration, August 31, 1837, delivered before the Phi Beta Kappa Society, Cambridge, Massachusetts.

See also EDUCATION

Gowns, and pecuniary foundations, though of towns of gold, can never countervail the least sentence or syllable of wit. Forget this, and our American colleges will recede in their public importance, whilst they grow richer every year.

"The American Scholar," repr. in *Emerson: Essays and Lectures*, ed. Joel Porte (1983).

Oration, August 31, 1837, delivered before the Phi Beta Kappa Society, Cambridge, Massachusetts.

See also EDUCATION

One of the benefits of a college education is, to show the boy its little avail.

"Culture," *The Conduct of Life* (1860).

See also EDUCATION

VIRTUE

In a virtuous action, I properly *am*; in a virtuous act, I add to the world; I plant into deserts conquered from Chaos and Nothing, and see the darkness receding on the limits of the horizon.

"Compensation," *Essays*, First Series (1841, repr. 1847).

The merit of those who fill a space in the world's history, who are borne forward, as it were, by the weight of thousands whom they lead, shed a perfume less sweet than do the sacrifices of private virtue.

"Historical Discourse at Concord," *Miscellanies* (1883, repr. 1904).

Speech, September 12, 1835, on the occasion of the second centennial anniversary of the town of Concord.

The less a man thinks or knows about his virtues, the better we like him.

"Spiritual Laws," *Essays,* First Series (1841, repr. 1847).

Virtue is the adherence in action to the nature of things, and the nature of things makes it prevalent. It consists in a perpetual substitution of being for seeming, and with sublime propriety God is described as saying, I AM.

"Spiritual Laws," *Essays,* First Series (1841, repr. 1847).

See also GOD

WEALTH AND THE WEALTHY

We honor the rich because they have externally the freedom, power, and grace which we feel to be proper to man, proper to us.

"History," *Essays,* First Series (1841, repr. 1847).

Without the rich heart, wealth is an ugly beggar.

"Manners," *Essays,* Second Series (1844).

Ah! if the rich were rich as the poor fancy riches!

"Nature," *Essays,* Second Series (1844).

The first wealth is health.

"Power," *The Conduct of Life* (1860).

See also HEALTH

*W*ISDOM

I find it more credible, since it is anterior information, that one man should *know heaven,* as the Chinese say, than that so many men should know the world.

"Character," *Essays,* Second Series (1844).

The wise through excess of wisdom is made a fool.

"Experience," *Essays,* Second Series (1844).

To finish the moment, to find the journey's end in every step of the road, to live the greatest number of good hours, is wisdom. It is not the part of men, but of fanatics, or of mathematicians, if you will, to say, that, the shortness of life considered, it is not worth caring whether for so short a duration we were sprawling in want, or sitting high. Since our office is with moments, let us husband them.

"Experience," *Essays,* Second Series (1844).

Emerson's solution to the Heroklitean dilemma of the succession of time is to give up the search for an overarching theme or undergirding transcendent substance, but to leap from moment to moment in a creative, fanciful frenzy.

See also LIFE

The first questions are always to be asked, and the wisest doctor is gravelled by the inquisitiveness of a child.

"Intellect," *Essays,* First Series (1841, repr. 1847).

See also CHILDREN

He who knows the most, he who knows what sweets and virtues are in the ground, the waters, the plants, the heavens, and how to come at these enchantments, is the rich and royal man.

"Nature," *Essays,* Second Series (1844).

The invariable mark of wisdom is to see the miraculous in the common.

Nature, ch. 8, (1836, revised and repr. 1849).

The lover of nature is he whose inward and outward senses are still truly adjusted to each other; who has retained the spirit of infancy even into the era of manhood.

Nature, ch. 1, (1836, revised and repr. 1849).

Emerson asserts here that we have both external and internal senses, thus he is attempting to move beyond the position of the English empiricists, especially John Locke. The notion of the wisdom of the infant recalls aspects of Eastern religious traditions, as well as Christianity, which proclaims that its Saviour entered the world as an infant.

See also NATURE

There is a certain wisdom of humanity which is common to the greatest men with the lowest, and which our ordinary education often labors to silence and obstruct.

"The Over-Soul," *Essays*, First Series (1841, repr. 1847).

See also EDUCATION

ᐤWᴏᴍᴇɴ

A beautiful woman is a practical poet, taming her savage mate, planting tenderness, hope and eloquence in all whom she approaches.

"Beauty," *The Conduct of Life* (1860).

Women stand related to beautiful nature around us, and the enamoured youth mixes their form with moon and stars, with woods and waters, and the pomp of summer. They heal us of awkwardness by their words and looks. We observe their intellectual influence on the most serious student. They refine and clear his mind: teach him to put a pleasing method into what is dry and difficult.

"Beauty," *The Conduct of Life* (1860).

Our American institutions have been friendly to her, and at this moment, I esteem it a chief felicity of this country, that it excels in women. A certain awkward consciousness of inferiority in men, may give rise to the new chivalry in behalf of Women's Rights. Certainly, let her be as much better placed in the laws and the social forms, as the most zealous reformer can ask, but I confide so entirely in her inspiring and musical nature, that I believe only herself can show us how she shall be served.

"Manners," *Essays*, Second Series (1844).

WORK

The day is always his, who works in it with serenity and great aims.

"The American Scholar," repr. In *Emerson: Essays and Lectures*, ed. Joel Porte (1983).

Oration, August 31, 1837, delivered before the Phi Beta Kappa Society, Cambridge, Massachusetts.

There is a great deal of self-denial and manliness in poor and middle-class houses, in town and country, that has not got into literature, and never will, but that keeps the earth sweet; that saves on superfluities, and spends on essentials; that goes rusty, and educates the boy; that sells the horse, but builds the school; works early and late, takes two looms in the factory, three looms, six looms, but pays off the mortgage on the paternal farm, and then goes back cheerfully to work again.

"Culture," *The Conduct of Life* (1860).

See also SIMPLICITY

Labor is God's education.

"Man the Reformer," *Nature, Addresses, and Lectures* (1849).

Speech, January 25, 1841, before the Mechanics' Apprentices' Library Association, Boston, Massachusetts.

See also EDUCATION

What we are, that only can we see. All that Adam had, all that Caesar could, you have and can do. Adam called his house, heaven and earth; Caesar called his house, Rome; you perhaps call yours, a cobbler's trade; a hundred acres of ploughed land; or a scholar's garret. Yet line for line and point for point, your dominion is as great as theirs, though without fine names. Build, therefore, your own world.

Nature, ch. 8, (1836, revised and repr. 1849).

If a man lose his balance, and immerse himself in any trades or pleasures for their own sake, he may be a good wheel or pin, but he is not a cultivated man.

"Prudence," *Essays*, First Series (1841, repr. 1847).

A man is relieved and gay when he has put his heart into his work and done his best; but what he has said or done otherwise shall give him no peace.

"Self-Reliance," *Essays*, First Series (1841, repr. 1847).

But do your thing, and I shall know you.

"Self-Reliance," *Essays*, First Series (1841 edition).

But do your work, and I shall know you. Do your work, and you shall reinforce yourself.

"Self-Reliance," *Essays*, First Series (1847).

There comes a time in every man's education when he arrives at the conviction that envy is ignorance; that imitation is suicide; that he must take himself for better for worse as his portion; that though the wide universe is full of good, no kernel of nourishing corn can come to him but through his toil bestowed on that plot of ground which is given him to till.

"Self-Reliance," *Essays*, First Series (1841, repr. 1847).

See also INDIVIDUALISM

Much of our reading, much of our labor, seems mere waiting: it was not that we were born for. Any other could do it as well or better. So little skill enters into these works, so little do they mix with the divine life, that it really signifies little what we do, whether we turn a grindstone, or ride, or run, or make fortune, or govern the state.

"The Transcendentalist," repr. in *The Portable Emerson*, ed. Carl Bode (1946, repr. 1981).

Speech, January 1842, at the Masonic Temple in Boston, repr. in *The Dial* (1843) and *Nature, Addresses, and Lectures* (1849).

*W*ORSHIP

And what greater calamity can fall upon a nation than the loss of worship? Then all things go to decay. Genius leaves the temple to haunt the senate or the market.

"The Divinity School Address," repr. in *The Portable Emerson*, ed. Carl Bode (1946, repr. 1981).

Address, July 17, 1838, delivered before the senior class in Divinity College, Cambridge.

See also RELIGION

Let me admonish you, first of all, to go alone; to refuse the good models, even those which are sacred in the imagination of men, and dare to love God without mediator or veil.

"The Divinity School Address," repr. in *The Portable Emerson*, ed. Carl Bode (1946, repr. 1981).

Delivered before the senior class in Divinity College, Cambridge, Sunday evening, July 15, 1838.

I am not so foolish as to declaim against forms. Forms are as essential as bodies; but to exalt particular forms, to adhere to one form a moment after it is outgrown, is unreasonable, and it is alien to the spirit of Christ.

"The Lord's Supper," *Miscellanies* (1883, repr. 1904).

Sermon, September 9, 1832, at the Second Church, Boston, Massachusetts.

See also RITUALS

The aspect of nature is devout. Like the figure of Jesus, she stands with bended head, and hands folded upon the breast. The happiest man is he who learns from nature the lesson of worship.

Nature, ch. 7, (1836, revised and repr. 1849).

See also NATURE

WRITERS AND WRITING

To-day I am full of thoughts and can write what I please. I see no reason why I should not have the same thought, the same power of expression, to-morrow. What I write, whilst I write it, seems the most natural thing in the world; but yesterday I saw a dreary vacuity in this direction in which now I see so much; and a month hence, I doubt not, I shall wonder who he was that wrote so many continuous pages. Alas for this infirm faith, this will not be strenuous, this vast ebb of a vast flow! I am God in nature; I am a weed by the wall.

"Circles," *Essays*, First Series (1841, repr. 1847).

See also CREATIVITY

Why need I volumes, if one word suffice?

"The Day's Ration," *Poems* (1847).

The ideal of silence and/or the single, precise word haunts much of Emerson's volumes of writing. One could argue that he was never able to answer this most central of Emersonian questions.

See also LANGUAGE

All writing comes by the grace of God, and all doing and having.

"Experience," *Essays*, Second Series (1844).

See also GOD

Best masters for the young writer and speaker are the fault-finding brothers and sisters at home who will not spare him, but will pick and cavil, and tell the odious truth.

The Journals of Ralph Waldo Emerson, vol. 10, ed. Edward Everett Emerson (1909–1914).

A wise writer will feel that the ends of study and composition are best answered by announcing undiscovered regions of thought, and so communicating, through hope, new activity to the torpid spirit.

Nature, ch. 8, (1836, revised and repr. 1849).

We write from aspiration and antagonism, as well as from experience. We paint those qualities which we do not possess.

"Prudence," *Essays*, First Series (1841, repr. 1847).

He that writes to himself writes to an eternal public. That statement only is fit to be made public, which you have come at in attempting to satisfy your own curiosity.

"Spiritual Laws," *Essays*, First Series (1841, repr. 1847).

The sentence must also contain its own apology for being spoken.

"Spiritual Laws," *Essays*, First Series (1841, repr. 1847).

Here again Emerson anticipates certain post-modern literary concepts.

A just thinker will allow full swing to his skepticism. I dip my pen in the blackest ink, because I am not afraid of falling into my inkpot.

"Worship," *The Conduct of Life* (1860).

*Y*OUTH

The delicious faces of children, the beauty of school-girls, "the sweet seriousness of sixteen," the lofty air of well-born, well-bred boys, the passionate histories in the looks and manners of youth and early manhood, and the varied power in all that well-known company that escort us through life,—we know how these forms thrill, paralyze, provoke, inspire, and enlarge us.

"Beauty," *The Conduct of Life* (1860).

See also LIFE

We see young men who owe us a new world, so readily and lavishly they promise, but they never acquit the debt; they die young and dodge the account: or if they live, they lose themselves in the crowd.

"Experience," *Essays,* Second Series (1844).

We are often made to feel that there is another youth and age than that which is measured from the year of our natural birth. Some thoughts always find us young, and keep us so. Such a thought is the love of the universal and eternal beauty.

"The Over-Soul," *Essays,* First Series (1841, repr. 1847).

Do not think the youth has no force, because he cannot speak to you and me. Hark! in the next room his voice is sufficiently clear and emphatic. It seems he knows how to speak to his contemporaries. Bashful or bold then, he will know how to make us seniors very unnecessary.

"Self-Reliance," *Essays,* First Series (1841, repr. 1847).